SACRED SONGS OF INDIA

Volume Seven

(HYMNS TO GAṆEŚA)

Books by V.K. SUBRAMANIAN

The Upanishads and the Bible

Introspection for India—A paradigm for progress

Sacred Songs of India (Volumes I, II, III, IV, V, VI)

Predictive Planets and Presaging Palms

Wondrous Whispers of Wisdom from Ancient India (Volumes I & II)

The Holistic Way to Health, Happiness and Harmony

Saundaryalahari

Maxims of Chanakya

The Indian Financial System

Sivanandalahari

Sri Rudra Prasna

The Great Ones (Volumes I & II)

Lali and Other Short Stories

Love Twigs

A Bond to Sorrow

SACRED SONGS OF INDIA

Volume Seven

(HYMNS TO GAṆEŚA)

V.K. SUBRAMANIAN

ABHINAV PUBLICATIONS
abhinav publications
NEW DELHI

Cataloging in Publication Data--DK
Courtesy: D.K. Agencies (P) Ltd. <docinfo@dkagencies.com>

Sacred songs of India / [translated by] V.K. Subramanian.
v. 7 cm.
Texts in Indian languages (Devanagari and roman); translation and introductory matter in English.
Selections from the lifework of mystic musician-saints of India; on love and devotion towards their favourite deities.
ISBN 8170174201

1. Sacred songs. 2. Hindu saints--Songs and music. 3. Bhajans. 4. Songs--India. 5. Devotional poetry, Indic--Translations into English. I. Subramanian, V. K. (Vadakaymadam Krishnier), 1930-
DDC 782.250 954 21

First published in India 2005

Publishers
Shakti Malik
Abhinav Publications
E-37, Hauz Khas
New Delhi-110016 (INDIA)
Phones: 26566387, 26562784, 26524658
Fax: 91-11-26857009
e-mail: shakti@nde.vsnl.net.in
Website: http//www.abhinavexports.com

ISBN 81-7017-420-1

Lasertypeset by
S.R. Enterprises
Lajpat Nagar-IV
New Delhi-110024 Ph.: 26236663

Printed at
D.K. Fine Art Press Pvt. Ltd.
Ashok Vihar, Delhi

To
my daughter Sunanda
who has looked after me for the last
so many years, like a truly devoted son

CONTENTS

Acknowledgements 11
Apologia 13
Introduction 15

1. Ancient Songs of Invocation of Gaṇeśa 19
2. Hymns by Agastya (2500 B.C.) 51
3. Hymns by Veda Vyasa (13th century B.C.) 63
4. Hymn by Tirumular (3rd century–5th century A.D.) 97
5. Hymn by Avvaiyar (7th century A.D.) 103
6. Hymns by Sankaracharya (788–820 A.D.) 123
7. Hymn by Jnaneswar (1275–1296 A.D.) 147
8. Hymns by Arunagirinathar (15th century A.D.) 153
9. Hymns by Purandharadasa (1484–1564 A.D.) 163
10. Hymn by Kanakadasa (16th century A.D.) 173
11. Hymn by Tulsidas (1532–1623 A.D.) 181
12. Hymns by Tukaram (1608–1650 A.D.) 187
13. Hymn by Eknath (1533–1606 A.D.) 195
14. Hymn by Samartha Ramadas (1608–1681 A.D.) 201
15. Hymns by Shahji Maharaja (1684–1710 A.D.) 207
16. Hymns by Oottukkadu Venkatasubba Iyer (1700–1765 A.D.) 215
17. Hymns by Tyagaraja (1767–1847 A.D.) 227
18. Hymns by Muttuswami Dikshitar (1775–1835 A.D.) 235
19. Hymns by Ramalinga Swamigal (1823–1874 A.D.) 259
20. Hymns by Nilakantha Sivan (1839–1900 A.D.) 285
21. Hymns by Narayana Guru (1856–1928 A.D.) 297

22. Hymns by Swami Brahmananda (1863-1922 A.D.) 309
23. Hymn by Harikesanallur Muthiah Bhagavatar (1877–1945 A.D.) 319
24. Hymns by Subramania Bharati (1882–1921 A.D.) 325
25. Hymns by Papanasam Sivan (1890–1973 A.D.) 345

KEY TO TRANSLITERATION AND PRONUNCIATION

Devanagari letter	Transli- terated as	Sounds like	Devanagari letter	Transli- terated as	Sounds like
अ	a	o in son	ट	ṭ	t in ten
आ	ā or aa	a in master	ठ	ṭh	th in anthill
इ	i	i in if	ड	ḍ	d in den
ई	ī or ee	ee in feel	ढ	ḍh	dh in childhood
उ	u	u in full	ण	ṇ	n in under
ऊ	ū or oo	oo in boot	त	t	t in French
ऋ	ṛ or ri	somewhat between r & ri	थ	th	th in thumb
			द	d	th in mother
ए	e	ay in May	ध	dh	th in breathe
ऐ	ai	y in my	न	n	n in not
ओ	o	o in oh	प	p	p in pen
औ	au	ow in now	फ	ph	ph in loophole
अः	ḥ	h in oh			
क	k	k in keen	ब	b	b in bag
ख	kh	ckh in blackhead	भ	bh	bh in abhor
ग	g	g in go	म	m	m in mother
घ	gh	gh in loghout	य	y	y in yard
ङ	ṅ	ṅ in singer	र	r	r in run
च	c	ch in chart	ल	l	l in luck
छ	ch	ch in chain	व	v	v in avert
ज	j	j in judge	श	ś	sh in reich
झ	jh	dgeh in hedgehog	ष	ṣ or sh	sh in show
ञ	ñ	n (somewhat) in French	स	s	s in sun
			ह	h	h in hot
			ळ	ḷ	ll in pull
			ऴ	zh	j in jean (French)

ACKNOWLEDGEMENTS

I would like to express my gratitude to the following friends but for whose help it would have been impossible to bring out this volume:

Late Sri R. Swaminathan whose help in transliteration continues to be visible, despite his sad demise.

Smt. B. Jayalakshmi who, despite her bad health, continues her valuable help in the translations of Tamil songs of Agastya, Avvaiyar, Ramalinga Swamigal and Subramania Bharati.

Smt. Krishna Veni Kasi Viswanath who made available the rare composition of Agastya, *Kāryasiddhimālai.*

Mrs. Nandini Kapdi I.A.A.S. for helping in the translation of the Kannada songs of Purandharadasa.

Mrs. Snehalata Datar for making available (with translation) Marathi songs of Jnaneswar, Eknath, Samartha Ramadas and Tukaram.

V.K. Subramanian

APOLOGIA

To make this compendium of sacred songs on Gaṇeśa as comprehensive and self-contained as possible, I have taken the liberty of including, in this volume, a few songs on Gaṇeśa composed by certain poet saints, though they found a place, along with their other compositions, in earlier volumes. Apologetically, I am listing these songs below for the benefit of my readers:

Sl. No.	Poet saint	Song	Raga	Vol.
1.	Veda Vyasa	*Ganesashtakam* from *Padma Purana*	Ragamalika	6
2.	Sankaracharya	*Ganesapancharatnam*	Ragamalika	6
3.	Jnaneswar	*Om namoji ādya*	Lalat	2
4.	Arunagirinathar	*Kaittala niraikani*	Nata	3
5.	Kanakadasa	*Nammamma Sarade*	Mohanam	3
6.	Eknath	*Omkar Swarupa*	Ahir Bhairavi	3
7.	Samartha Ramadas	*Sukhakarta dukhaharta*	Jogiya	5
8.	Shahji Maharaja	*Ceta Cintaya*	Suddha Bandhuvarali	6
9.	Muttuswami Dikshitar	*Vātapi Ganapatim*	Hamsadhwani	2
		Vallabhanayakasya	Begada	2
		Srimuladharmacakra	Sri	2
10.	Subramania Bharati	*Karpaga Vinayaka*	Nata	2
11.	Papanasam Sivan	*Mūladhara mūrti*	Hamsadhwani	2

V.K. Subramanian

INTRODUCTION

This series of *Sacred Songs of India,* comprising the devotional lyrics of the mystic saints from different regions of India and different periods of its history are hymns of praise to God, in diverse manifestations of Divinity.

God is Spirit and cannot be easily conceived except through images and symbols, which have evolved over centuries, out of myth and legend, and mystic vision and experience of spiritually evolved sages.

In India, six manifestations of God are worshipped with love and devotion. These are:

1. *Gaṇeśa,* the Darling Deity
2. *Krishna,* who is also *Rāma,* incarnation of Vishnu
3. *Śiva,* the Auspicious One
4. *Śakti,* the Divine Mother
5. *Kumara* or *Subramania,* the embodiment of youth, beauty and valour
6. Sun, the giver of life-sustaining light.

Different spiritual aspirants or mystics choose the image which turns them on spiritually, enabling them to attain blissful beatitude.

Thus, in Sacred Songs of India Volume One, I presented the songs of ten mystics who were intoxicated with God in the form of *Krishna* or *Rama.*

Subsequent volumes have dealt with saints obsessed with other images like *Siva, Sakti, Subramania* etc.

In this volume I am presenting the songs of the mystics on *Gaṇeśa,* the Darling Deity.

The hymns included date back to the Vedic period (2500 B.C.) and subsequent periods extending upto the modern age, viz. the twentieth century.

At this stage, I have to make certain clarifications about image worship in general and the image of *Gaṇeśa* in particular.

As Houston Smith observes in his book, *World's Religions, "It is obtuse to confuse Hinduism's images with idolatry, and their multiplicity with polytheism. They are runways from which the sense-encumbered human spirit can rise for its "flight of the alone to the Alone".*

"A symbol such as a multi-armed image can represent God's power; myths can plumb depths that are closed to the intellect; parables and legends present ideals in ways that make hearers long to embody them.

"The value of these things lies in their power to recall our minds from the world's distractions to the thought of God and God's love".

The six (*i*nterchangeable and interconnected) images of God mentioned earlier have inspired hundreds of poet sages to pour out their love and devotion in ecstatic poetry.

They have also enabled many to realise God.

The image of *Gaṇeśa,* the elephant-faced infant has had a universal appeal and God is worshipped in this form by all, before commencing any important work or conducting any important function like wedding or other rituals.

God, in this form, is supposed to destroy all obstacles which stand in the way of successful achievement of tasks.

The hymns to *Gaṇeśa* included in this volume span over twenty centuries.

They have been selected from the *Vedas*, the *Upanishads*, the *Puranas* and from the works of sages and mystic saints from all regions of India.

Thus the hymns are in many languages:

Sanskrit, Hindi, Kannada, Marathi, Tamil, Telugu and *Malayalam.*

These hymns are an expression of spiritual experience, an outpouring of pure love and devotion to God, inspired by the patently grotesque and paradoxical image of the Elephant-faced Darling Deity, which represented, in the mystic vision of the sages, the *Pranava* sound, *AUM,* the symbol of creation, protection and destruction and whose childlike-giving goodness endeared their hearts.

Loving God intensely is the spiritual path of devotees who seek to realise God through *Bhakti* (devotion).

Different facets of this love are adopted by mystics:

1. *Bridal mysticism of treating God as the lover or beloved*

The image of God as Krishna, the eternal lover caters to this attitude of the devotee, as also the image of *Kumara* or *Subramania,* the embodiment of youth, beauty and valour.

2. *Treating God as a parent*

The images of God as *Siva* or *Sakti,* the Divine Mother fulfil this craving.

3. *Treating God as a child and expressing parental love*

The image of the infant deity, Gaṇeśa answers to this need as also the image of child Krishna.

4. *Treating God as a friend in need*

5. *Treating God as a Master*

The last two attitudes are possible with all images of God.

The adorable appeal of *Gaṇeśa* can be understood when one remembers that elephant is an object of perennial charm, which we, especially children, never tire of looking at. (The other two similar objects are the moon and the ocean!*)

Gaṇeśa evokes the child in the devotee, while He himselfis in child form.

He is the symbol of AUM, the source of all creation. Yet he is not only the root of creation but of creativity as well.

---

*I am indebted to the late Sage of Kanchi, Paramacharya, for this beautiful thought.

The Vedic chant extols Him as the Poet of poets.

Gaṇeśa represents unalloyed bliss, goodness and knowledge.

Let us dip into the ocean of devotion, bequeathed to us by the sages, centred on this beloved image of God, and savour the resultant satisfaction.

V.K. Subramanian

ANCIENT SONGS OF INVOCATION OF GAṆEŚA

Sl. No.	Song	Raga
1.	Suklāmbaradharam Vishnum	Yaman
2.	Gajānanam Bhūtagaṇādi sevitam	Nāṭa
3.	Vakratuṇḍa Mahākāya	Mohanam
4.	Caturbhujam Mahākāyam	Hindolam
5.	Sarvavighnaharam	Śuddhasāveri
6.	Guṇātītamānam	Hamsadhwani
7.	Sivatanaya variṣṭam	Sindhubhairavi
8.	Yam Brahmavedāntavido	Bandhuvarāli
9.	Ekadantam Mahākāyam	Tilang
10.	Agajānanapadmārkam	Gambhīra Nāṭai
11.	Dh yāyennityam Gaṇeśam	Behāg
12.	Yasya dviradavaktrādyāḥ	Sahānā
13.	Namo Namo Gaṇeśāya	Toḍi
14.	Gajavadanamacintyam	Kāpi
15.	Gajānanam Ganapatim	Rītigowḷa
16.	Invocation of 16 names	Madhyamāvati
17.	Prayer to Gaṇeśa from Rig Veda	Yaman
18.	Ganapati Atharvasirsa Upanishad	Yaman

राग: यमन — Raga: Yaman

1. शुक्लाम्बरधरं विष्णुं
शशिवर्णं चतुर्भुजं।
प्रसन्नवदनं ध्यायेत्
सर्वविघ्नोपशान्तये।।

śuklāmbaradharam viṣṇum
śaśivarṇam caturbhujam
prasannavadanam dhyāyet
sarvavighnopaśāntaye.

राग: नाट — Raga: Nāṭa

2. गजाननं भूतगणाधिसेवितं
कपित्थजम्बूफलसारभक्षितं।
उमासुतं शोकविनाशकारणं
नमामि विघ्नेश्वरपादपङ्कजं।।

gajānanam bhūtagaṇādhisevitam
kapitthajambūphalasārabhakṣitam
umāsutam śokavināśakāraṇam
namāmi vighneśvarapādapankajam.

1. Suklāmbaradharam vishnum

Let us meditate on the pleasant faced Lord,
who wears a white robe, is omnipresent,
whose colour is like that of the moon,
who has four arms,
so that all the obstacles can be banished.

2. Gajānanam bhūtagaṇādisevitam

I bow to the lotus feet of Vighneswara, the Lord of obstacles,
who is elephant-faced, and is served by the elements and spiritual attendants,
who eats the essence of the wood apple and the rose apple,
who is the son of Umā, the Divine Mother,
and who is the cause for destruction of all sorrow.

रागः मोहनं — Raga: Mohanam

3. वक्रतुण्ड महाकाय
कोटिसूर्यसमप्रभः।
निर्विघ्नंकुरु मे देव
सर्वकार्येषु सर्वदा।।

vakratuṇḍa mahākāya
koṭisūryasamaprabhaḥ
nirvighnam kuru me deva
sarvakāryeṣu sarvadā.

रागः हिन्दोलं — Raga: Hindolam

4. चतुर्भुजं महाकायं गजवक्त्रं सुखाकरं।
भक्तानां वरदं ध्याये महागणपतिं विभुं।।

caturbhujam mahākāyam gajavaktram
sukhākaram
bhaktānām varadam dhyāye mahāgaṇapatim
vibhum.

3. Vakratuṇḍa mahākāya

O Lord, with the curving trunk and the huge body!
Your splendour is equal to that of a million suns,
Always make all my enterprises
free of obstacles!

4. Caturbhujam mahākāyam

I meditate on the great Ganapati,
the lord of spiritual attendants,
who is four-armed, has a huge body,
is elephant-faced and is the creator of contentment,
who grants boons to devotees,
and is all-pervading.

रागः शुद्धसावेरि — Raga: Śuddhasāveri

5. सर्वविघ्नहरं देवं
सर्वविघ्न विवर्जितं।
सर्वसिद्धि प्रदातारं
वन्देहं गणनायकम्।।

sarvavighnaharam devam
sarvavighna vivarjitam
sarvasiddhipradātāram
vandeham gaṇanāyakam.

रागः हंसध्वनि — Raga: Hamsadhwani

6. गुणातीत मानं चिदानन्दरूपं
चिदाभासकं सर्वगं ज्ञानगम्यम्।
मुनिध्येयमाकाशरूपं परेशं
परब्रह्मरूपं गणेशं भजेम।।

guṇātītamānam cidānandarūpam
cidābhāsakam sarvagam jnānagamyam
munidhyeyamākāśarūpam pareśam
parabrahmarūpam gaṇeśam bhajema.

5. Sarvavighnaharam

I bow to the Leader of Ganas, the spiritual attendants,
the Lord who removes all obstacles,
who is devoid of any obstacle,
who gives success in all undertakings.

6. Guṇātītamānaṃ

Let us worship that Lord Ganesa,
who is the embodiment of the Supreme God,
who is beyond all attributes,
whose form is consciousness-bliss,
who shines in consciousness,
is present everywhere and in everything,
who is the goal of all knowledge,
who is meditated upon by sages,
whose form is the ether,
the Supreme Lord!

रागः सिंधुभैरवि — Raga: Sindhubhairavi

7. शिवतनयवरिष्टं सर्वकल्याणमूर्तिं
परशुदशनकन्धे शोभितं मोदकेन।
अरुणकुसुममालाव्यालम्भोजनेत्रं
मम हृदय निवासं श्रीगणेशं नमामि।।

śivatanaya variṣṭam sarvakalyāṇamūrtim
paraśudaśanakandhe śobhitam modakena
aruṇakusumamālāvyālambhojanetram
mama hṛdayanivāsam śrī gaṇeśam namāmi.

रागः बन्धुवरालि — Raga: Bandhuvarāli

8. यं ब्रह्मवेदान्तविदो वदन्ति
परं प्रधानं पुरुषं तथान्ये।
विश्वोद्गते कारणमीश्वरं वा
तस्मै नमो विघ्नविनाशनाय।।

yam brahmavedāntavido vadanti
param pradhānam puruṣam tathānye
viśvodgate kāraṇamīśvaram vā
tasmai namo vighnavināśanāya.

7. Sivatanayavariṣṭam

I offer prostrations to the auspicious Lord Ganesa,
the lord of spiritual attendants,
the eldest son of Siva,
is the embodiment of all auspicious virtues,
whose shoulder is touched by the axe,
who shines with the rice cake,
who wears a garland of crimson flowers and snakes,
whose eyes are like the lotus and
who ever resides in my heart!

8. Yam Brahmavedāntavido

Prostrations to that destroyer of obstacles,
who is mentioned as God by knowers of Vedanta,
and as the supreme primordial person by others,
or as the Lord who is the cause for the origin of the universe.

राग: तिलंग — Raga: Tilang

9. एकदन्तं महाकायं
तप्तकाञ्चन सन्निभं।
लम्बोदरं विरूपाक्षं
वन्देऽहं गणनायकं।।

ekadantam mahākāyam
taptakāñcana sannibham
lambodaram virūpākṣam
vandeham gaṇanāyakam.

राग: गंभीर नाटै — Raga: Gambhīra Nāṭai

10. अगजाननपद्मार्कं
गजानन महन्निशं।
अनेकदं तं भक्तानां
एकदन्तमुपास्महे।।

agajānanapadmārkam
gajānanamahanniśam
anekadam tam bhaktānām
ekadantamupāsmahe.

9. Ekadantam mahākāyam

I bow to the Leader of Ganas, the spiritual attendants,
who has a single tusk,*
who is big bodied
whose splendour is like that of molten gold,
who has a big belly,
and has unusual eyes.

10. Agajānanapadmārkam

I worship, day and night,
that Lord with the single tusk,
who is like the sun to the lotus,
which is the face of the mountain-born Divine Mother,
the elephant-faced one,
who grants many things to devotees.

*There are two myths regarding the single tusk of Ganesa. The first is that in fighting a demon called Gajamukha, Ganesa had to use one of the two tusks as a weapon. The second myth is that for writing the epic Mahabharata dictated by the sage Veda Vyasa, Ganesa, the scribe broke one of his tusks and used it as a pen to write the epic.

रागः बेहाग

Raga: Behāg

11. ध्यायेन्नित्यं गणेशं परमगुणयुतं
ध्यानसंस्थं त्रिनेत्रं
एकं देवं त्वनेकं परमसुखयुतं
देवदेवं प्रसन्नं
शुण्डादण्डाद्यगण्डोद्गलितमदजलो
ल्लोलमत्तालिमालं
श्रीमन्तं विघ्नराजं सकलसुखकरं
श्री गणेशं नमामि।

dhyāyennityam gaṇeśam paramaguṇayutam
dhyānasamstham trinetram
ekam devam tvanekam paramasukhayutam
devadevam prasannam
śuṇḍādaṇḍādyagaṇḍodgalitamadajalo
llolamattālimālam
śrīmantam vighnarājam sakalasukhakaram
śrī gaṇeśam namāmi.

रागः सहाना

Raga: Sahānā

12. यस्य द्विरदवक्त्राद्याः
पारिषद्याः परश्शतं
विघ्नं निघ्नन्ति सततं
विश्वक्षेनं तमाश्रये।

yasya dviradavaktrādyāḥ
pāriṣadyāḥ paraśśatam
vighnam nighnanti satatam
viśvakṣenam tamāśraye.

11. Dhyāyennityam gaṇeśam

Let us daily meditate on Ganesa,
who has many supreme qualities,
who is located by meditation, and has three eyes,
the unique Lord, who is full of many facets of supreme bliss,
who is the lord of angels, is pleasant faced,
who is surrounded by an array of bees eager to taste the rut juice flowing from his temples,
who is full of auspiciousness,
the ruler of obstacles,
who creates total happiness.

12. Yasya dviradavaktrādyāḥ

I seek refuge in that omnipresent Lord,
from whose elephant mouth, hundreds of warriors come out
and always destroy obstacles.

रागः तोडि — Raga: Toḍi

13. नमो नमो गणेशाय
नमस्ते शिवसूनवे
निर्विघ्नं कुरु देवेश
नमामि त्वां गणाधिप।।

namo namo gaṇeśāya
namaste śivasūnave
nirvighnam kuru deveśa
namāmi tvām gaṇādhipa.

रागः कापि — Raga: Kāpi

14. गजवदनमचिन्त्यं तीक्ष्णदन्तं त्रिनेत्रं
बृहदुदरमशेषं पूतरूपं पुराणं।
अमरवरसुपूज्यं रक्तवर्णं सुरेशं
पशुपतिसुतमीशं विघ्नराजं नमामि।।

gajavadanamacintyam tīkṣṇadantam trinetram
bṛhadudaramaśeṣam pūtarūpam purāṇam
amaravarasupūjyam raktavarṇam sureśam
paśupatisutamīśam vighnarājam namāmi.

13. Namo namo gaṇeśāya

Prostrations and prostrations to Lord Ganesa,
Prostrations to the son of Siva,
O Lord of angels! See that there are no obstacles (on my path),
I prostrate before you,
O Lord of spiritual attendants!

14. Gajavadanamacintyam

I prostrate before the Lord of obstacles,
Who is elephant faced,
who is unimaginable,
has sharp tusk, and three eyes!
Who has a big belly, who outlasts everything,
who has a pure form,
who is very ancient,
who is well worshipped by angels,
who is crimson coloured,
the Lord of celestials,
the Lord, who is the son of Siva, the Lord of all creatures.

रागः रीतिगौळ

Raga: Rītigowḷa

15. गजाननं गणपतिं
गुणानामालयं परं
तं देवं गिरिजासूनुं
वन्द्येहं अमरार्चितं।

gajānanam gaṇapatim
guṇānāmālayam param
tam devam girijāsūnum
vandyeham amarārcitam.

15. Gajānanam gaṇapatim

I worship that Lord,
who is elephant faced,
who is the Lord of Ganas, the spiritual attendants,
who is the abode of good qualities,
the Supreme One,
the son of Girija, the Divine Mother, born of the mountain,
who is worshipped by angels.

राग: मध्यमावति

Raga: Madhyamāvati

16. 1. सुमुखाय नमः
Sumukhāya namaḥ

2. एकदन्ताय नमः
Ekadantāya namaḥ

3. कपिलाय नमः
Kapilāya namaḥ

4. गजकर्णकाय नमः
Gajakarṇakāya namaḥ

5. लम्बोदराय नमः
Lambodarāya namaḥ

6. विकटाय नमः
Vikaṭāya namaḥ

7. विघ्नराजाय नमः
Vighnarājāya namaḥ

8. विनायकाय नमः
Vināyakāya namaḥ

9. धूमकेतवे नमः
Dhūmaketave namaḥ

10. गणाध्यक्षाय नमः
Gaṇādhyakṣāya namaḥ

11. फालचन्द्राय नमः
Phālachandrāya namaḥ

12. गजाननाय नमः
Gajānanāya namaḥ

13. वक्रतुण्डाय नमः
Vakratuṇḍāya namaḥ

16. Invocation of the sixteen names of Gaṇésa
    Prostrations to:
    1. The pleasant-faced One!
    2. The Lord with the single tusk!
    3. The crimson coloured One!
    4. The One with elephant ears!
    5. The One with the big belly!
    6. The huge One!
    7. The Conqueror of obstacles!
    8. The One who has no leader above him!
    9. The One who exists as fire!
    10. The Lord of spiritual attendants!
    11. The One who has the moon on the forehead!
    12. The elephant-faced One!
    13. The One who has a curving trunk!

14. शूर्पकर्णाय नमः
    Śūrpakarṇāya namaḥ

15. हेरम्बाय नमः
    Herambāya namaḥ

16. स्कन्ध पूर्वजाय नमः
    Skandha pūrvajāya namaḥ

14. The One who has ears resembling winnowing mats!

15. The One who is heroic!

16. The elder brother of Subrahmania!

17. ऋग्वेदे अन्तर्गतं गणेशस्तवं

राग: यमन — Raga: Yaman

ॐ गणानां त्वा गणपतिम् हवामहे
कविं कवीनामुपमश्रवस्तमम्।
ज्येष्ठराजं ब्रह्मणां ब्रह्मणस्पत
आ नः शृण्वन्नूतिभिस्सीद सादनम्।।
महा गणपतये नमः।

om gaṇānām tvā gaṇapatim havāmahe
kavim kavīnāmupamaśravastamam
jyeṣṭharājam brahmaṇām brahmaṇaspata
ā naḥ śṛṇvannūtibhissīdasādanam
mahāgaṇapataye namaḥ.

18. श्री गणपति अथर्वशीर्षोपनिषद्

राग: यमन — Raga: Yaman

ॐ नमस्ते गणपतये। त्वमेव
प्रत्यक्षं तत्त्वमसि। त्वमेव केवलं
कर्तासि। त्वमेव केवलं धर्तासि।
त्वमेव केवलं हर्तासि। त्वमेव सर्वं
खल्विदं ब्रह्मासि। त्वं साक्षादात्मासि
नित्यम्।।

om namaste gaṇapataye tvameva
pratyakṣam tattvamasi tvameva kevalam
kartāsi tvameva kevalam dhartāsi
tvameva kevalam hartāsi tvameva sarvam
khalvidam brahmāsi tvam sākṣādātmāsi
nityam.

17. Prayer to Lord Gaṇeśa from the Vedas (Rig Veda)

Om Gaṇānām tvā gaṇapatim

We invoke you, the Lord of Ganas!
the Poet of poets, the Supreme standard bearer in learning!
the Eldest Ruler, the Lord of creators!
Please come and hear our hymns and bless our residences!
Prostrations to the Great Lord of Ganas!

18. Śrī Gaṇapati Atharvaśīrṣa Upaniṣad

Aum

Prostrations to Ganapati, the Lord of spiritual attendants
You alone are the patent Truth (That thou art)!
You alone are the Creator of the cosmos!
You alone are the Protector of the cosmos!
You alone are the Destroyer of the cosmos!
You alone are this omnipresent Reality!
You are really the immortal Self!
You are eternal!

ऋतं वच्मि। सत्यं वच्मि।।

ritam vacmi satyam vacmi.

अव त्वं माम्। अव वक्तारम्।
अव श्रोतारम्। अव दातारम्।
अव धातारम्। अवानूचानमव शिष्यम्।
अव पश्चात्तात्। अव पुरस्तात्।
अवोत्तरात्तात्। अव दक्षिणात्तात्।
अव चोर्ध्वात्तात्। अवाधरात्तात्।
सर्वतो मां पाहि पाहि समन्तात्।।

ava tvam mām ava vaktāram
ava śrotāram ava dātāram
ava dhātāram avānūcānamava śiṣyam
ava paścāttāt ava purastāt avo-
ttarāttāt ava dakṣiṇāttāt ava
cordhvāttāt avādharāttāt sarvato
mām pāhi pāhi samantāt.

त्वं वाङ्मयस्त्वं चिन्मयः। त्वमान-
न्दमयस्त्वं ब्रह्ममयः। त्वं सच्चिदान-
न्दाद्वितीयोसि। त्वं प्रत्यक्षं ब्रह्मासि।
त्वं ज्ञानमयो विज्ञानमयोसि।।

tvam vāngmayastvam cinmayaḥ tvamāna-
ndamayastvam brahmamayaḥ tvam saccidāna-
ndādvitīyosi tvam pratyakṣam brahmāsi
tvam jnānamayo vijnānamayosi.

I speak what is apt. I speak the truth.

You protect me.
Protect the speaker.
Protect the listener.
Protect the donor.
Protect the bearer.
Protect the teacher and the student.
Protect before and after.
Protect from the north and the south.
Protect from above and below.
Always protect me, protect me.

You pervade all sound.
You are pure consciousness.
You are bliss. You are God.
You are none other than existence, consciousness bliss.
You are the perceptible God.
You are the embodiment of knowledge and wisdom.

सर्वं जगदिदं त्वत्तो जायते।
सर्वं जगदिदं त्वत्तस्तिष्ठति। सर्वं
जगदिदं त्वयि लयमेष्यति। सर्वं
जगदिदं त्वयि प्रत्येति। त्वं भूमिरा-
पोनलोनिलो नभः। त्वं चत्वारि
वाक्पदानि।।

sarvam jagadidam tvatto jāyate
sarvam jagadidam tvattastiṣṭhati sarvam
jagadidam tvayi layameṣyati sarvam
jagadidam tvayi pratyeti. tvam bhūmirā-
ponalonilo nabhaḥ tvam catvāri
vākpadāni.

त्वं गुणत्रयातीतः। त्वं देहत्रया-
तीतः। त्वमवस्थात्रयातीतः। त्वं
कालत्रयातीतः। त्वं मूलाधारस्थितो-
सि नित्यम्। त्वं शक्तित्रयात्मकः। त्वां
योगिनो ध्यायन्ति नित्यम्। त्वं ब्रह्मा
त्वं विष्णुस्त्वं रुद्रस्त्वमिन्द्रस्त्वमग्निस्त्वं
वायुस्त्वं सूर्यस्त्वं चंद्रमास्त्वं ब्रह्मभू-र्भुवः स्वरोम्।।

tvam guṇatrayātītaḥ tvam dehatrayā-
tītaḥ tvamavasthātrayātītaḥ tvam
kālatrayātītaḥ tvam mūlādhārasthito-
si nityam tvam śaktitrayātmakaḥ tvām
yogino dhyāyanti nityam tvam brahmā tvam
viṣṇustvam rudrastvamindrastvamagnistvam
vāyustvam sūryastvam candramāstvam brahmabhū-
rbhuvaḥ svarom.

All this universe is born out of you.
All this universe stands sustained in you.
All this universe dissolves into you.
All this universe returns to you.
You are earth, water, fire, air and ether (space).
You distinguish the four categories of people.

You are beyond the three qualities (sattva, rajas and tamas).
You are beyond the three types of bodies (gross, subtle, causal).
You are beyond the three states (waking, dream, sleep).
You are beyond the three periods of time (past, present, future).
You are ever located in the *Mūlādhāra* cakra.
You are the embodiment of the three types of power (will, knowledge, action).
Sages always meditate on you.
You are Brahma, Vishnu, Rudra (the Creator, Preserver, Destroyer).
You are Indra, the Chief of celestials!
You are Fire, Air, Sun, Moon.
You are God!
You are earth, ether and heaven.
You are the *Pranava* sound: *AUM*.

गणादिं पूर्वमुच्चार्य वर्णादिं तदन-
न्तरम्। अनुस्वारः परतरः। अर्धेन्दुल-
सितम्। तारेण रुद्रम्। एतत्तव
मनुस्वरूपम्। गकारः पूर्वरूपम्।
अकारो मध्यमरूपम्। अनुस्वरश्चान्त-
रूपम्। बिन्दुरुत्तररूपम्। नादः
सन्धानम्। समृहिता सन्धिः। सैंषा
गणेशविद्या। गणक ऋषिः। निचृद्-
गायत्री छन्दः। गणपतिर्देवता। ॐ
गं गणपतये नमः।।

gaṇādim pūrvamuccārya varṇādim tadana-
ntaram anusvāraḥ parataraḥ ardhendula-
sitam tāreṇa rudram etattava
manusvarūpam gakāraḥ pūrvarūpam
akāro madhyamarūpam anusvaraścānta-
rūpam binduruttararūpam nādaḥ
sandhānam samhitā sandhiḥ saiṣā
gaṇeśavidyā gaṇaka ṛṣiḥ nicṛd-
gāyatrī chandaḥ gaṇapatirdevatā om
gam gaṇapataye namaḥ.

एकदन्ताय विद्महे वक्रतुण्डाय
धीमहि। तन्नो दन्तिः प्रचोदयात्।।

ekadantāya vidmahe vakratuṇḍāya
dhīmahi tanno dantiḥ pracodayāt.

First uttering the first letter of the word *Gana, Ga,*
I utter the nasal sound which follows and shines like the crescent moon.
This is your form
Ga is the first part,
A is the middle part,
The nasal sound is the final part.
Combining all the sounds, I utter: *Gam*
This is the *Gaṇeśa* mantra
(Of this mantra), *Ganaka* is the Rishi*
Nṛcṛt gāyatri is the *chandas,*
Ganapati is the Deity
Prostrations to Gaṇeśa.

I meditate on the Lord with one tusk.
I meditate on the Lord with the curved trunk.
Let the elephant-faced Lord illuminate and inspire me!

---

*In the chanting of secret mantras, in India, for each mantra, a *Rishi* (sage), *Chandas* (rhythm) and a *Devata* (Deity) are specified.

एकदन्तं चतुर्हस्तं पाशमङ्कुश-
धारिणम्। रदं च वरदं हस्तैर्बिभ्राणं
मूषकध्वजम्। रक्तं लम्बोदरं शूर्पकर्णकं
रक्त वाससं रक्त गन्धानुलिप्ताङ्गं
रक्तपुष्पैः सुपूजितम्। भक्तानुकंपिनं
देवं जगत्कारणमच्युतम्। आविर्भूतं
च सृष्टयादौ प्रकृतेः पुरुषात् परम्।
एवं ध्यायति यो नित्यं स योगी
योगिनां वरः।।

ekadantam caturhastam pāśamankuśa-
dhāriṇam radam ca varadam
hastairvibhrāṇam
mūṣakadhwajam raktam lambodaram
śūrpakarṇakam
raktavāsasam raktagandhānuliptāṅgam
raktapuṣpaiḥ supūjitam bhaktānukampinam
devam jagatkāraṇamacyutam āvirbhūtam
ca sṛṣṭyādau prakṛteḥ puruṣāt param
evam dhyāyati yo nityam sa yogī
yoginām varaḥ.

नमो व्रातपतये। नमो गणपतये।
नमः प्रथमपतये। नमस्तेस्तु लम्बो-
दरायैकदन्ताय विघ्ननाशिने शिव-
सुताय श्रीवरदमूर्तये नमः।।

namo vrātapataye namo gaṇapataye
namaḥ prathamapataye namastestu lambo-
darāyaikadantāya vighnanāśine śiva-
sutāya śrīvaradamūrtaye namaḥ.

He is One with a single tusk and has four hands.
He holds the noose and the goad.
With his hands, he holds the tusk and gives blessing.
He is crimson hued and has a big belly.
His ears resemble a winnowing mat.
He wears a red garment.
His limbs are covered with red sandal paste.
He is worshipped with red flowers.
He is compassionate to his devotees.
He is the cause of the cosmos. He is imperishable.
He manifested himself before creation.
He is superior to *Purusha* and *Prakṛti.*
He who meditates on Him thus becomes the Yogi of yogis.

Prostrations to Lord of multitudes!
Prostrations to the Lord of attendants!
Prostrations to the primordial Lord!
Prostrations to the Lord with the big belly!
Prostrations to the Lord with one tusk!
Prostrations to the Lord who destroys obstacles!
Prostrations to the son of Siva!
Prostrations to the auspicious Lord in the boon granting form!

AGASTYA'S HYMNS TO GAṆEŚA

	Hymn	*Raga*
1.	Bandhamakattrum	Hamsadhwani
2.	Ulakam muzhutum	Hamsadhwani
3.	Idarkal muzhutum	Dhanyāsi
4.	Mūrtiyāki talamāki	Dhanyāsi
5.	Ceyyum vinaiyin	Mohanam
6.	Vedam alantum	Mohanam
7.	Mannin or aingunamāki	Suruti
8.	Pāśa arivum paśu arivum	Suruti

AGASTYA

AGASTYA (2500 B.C.)

There are so many myths and legends about Agastya in the puranas and the epics, one would have doubted his physical existence but for his works which are very much with us.

Sage Agastya, who was dwarfish in appearance, is considered thc doyen of Tamil mystics and the father of the Tamil language. He is to the Tamil language what Panini was to Sanskrit.

The Tamil grammar *Tolkāpyam*, one of the oldest grammars in the world, was written by one of the twelve disciples of Agastya. The songs on Ganesa composed by Agastya in Tamil are taken from his work *"Kāryasiddhi Malai"*.

Agastya is famous for teaching the *"Āditya Hṛdaya"* mantra to Sri Rama on the eve of his battle with the demon Ravana. Rama is believed to have won a victory because of the power of the prayer to the Sun taught by Agastya. Even today millions recite this prayer to achieve success and get rid of eye problems.

Agastya's songs on Ganesa included in this volume are also believed to ensure success in all undertakings.

Kāryasiddhimalai literally means "garland (of songs) which ensures success in undertakings".

Other works attributed to Agastya are:

1. *Agastya Gita* (in the Varahapurana)
2. *Agastya Samhita* (in Skandapurana)
3. *Siva Samhita* (in Bhaskara Samhita)
4. *Dvaida Nirnaya Tantra*.

कार्यसिद्धिमाला (अगस्त्य विरचितं)

राग: हंसध्वनि Raga: Hamsadhwani

1. बन्धमकट्ट्रूं अनन्तगुणपरप्पुं एवन्पाल् उदिक्कुमो
इन्तउलकुं एवनिडत्तिल् ईण्टियिरुन्तु चुरक्कुमो
सन्तमरै आगमङ्गलान्तं एवन्पाल् तकवरुमो
अन्त इरैयां गणपतियै अन्पुकूरतोऴुकिन्राम्।

bandhamakaṭṭrum anantaguṇaparappum evanpāl udikkumo
intaulakum evaniḍattil eenṭiyiruntu curakkumo
santamarai āgamangalāntam evanpāl takavarumo
anta iraiyām gaṇapatiyai anpu kūratozhukinrām.

राग: हंसध्वनि Raga: Hamsadhwani

2. उलकं मुऴुतुं नीक्कमऱ् ओनऱाय् निर्कुं पोरुळ् एवन अव
उलकिल् पिऱक्कुं विकारङ्कळ् उऱातमेलां ओळियावन्
उलकं पुरियुं विनैप्पयनै ऊट्टुं कळैक्कण् एवन् अन्त
उलकमुतलै गणपतियै उवन्तुं शरणमडैकिन्ऱाम्।

ulakam muzhutum nīkkamar onrāy nirkum poruḷ evan ava
ulakil piṛakkum vikāraṇkaḷ urātamelām oḷiyāvan
ulakam puriyum vinaippayanai ūṭṭum kaḷaikkaṇ evan anta
ulakamutalai gaṇapatiyai uvantum śaraṇa-maḍaikinrām.

Karyasiddhimala of Agastya

1. Bandhamakattrum

I bow, with great love, to that Lord, Ganapati, the Master of spiritual attendants,
from whom rise limitless qualities which dispel bondage,
from whom this world has manifested,
from whom have risen the resonant Vedas and other scriptures and all arts.

2. Ulakam muzhutum

I seek refuge, with delight, in that primal cause of the world, Ganapati,
the Lord of spiritual attendants,
who is the single reality pervading all beings everywhere, the radiant Lord,
who is above all (conflicting) emotions,
who makes living beings undergo the results of their actions.

रागः धन्यासि

Raga: Dhanyāsi

3. इडर्कळ् मुऴ़ुतुं एवनरुळाल् एरि वीऴ़ुं पञ्चेनमायुं
तोडरुं उयिर्कळ् एवनरुळाल् सुरर् वाऴ़पतियुंउरचेय्युं
कटवुळ् मतलोर् कूरिन्रि करुमं एवनाल् मुट्विुरुं अत्
ततवुं मरुप्पु गणपतियै शरणं शरणमडैकिन्राम्।

iḍarkaḷ muzhutum evanaṛuḷāl eri vīzhum pan-
cenamāyum
toḍarum uyirkaḷ evanaṛuḷāl surar vāzhapatiyumur-
ceyyum
kaṭavuḷ matalor kūriṇri karumam evanāl muṭivurum at
tatavum maṛuppu gaṇapatiyai śaraṇam śaraṇa-
maḍaikinrām.

रागः धन्यासि

Raga: Dhanyāsi

4. मूर्त्तियाकि तलमाकि मुन्नीर् गंगै मुतलान
तीर्थमाकि अरिन्तरिया तिरत्तिनालुं उयिक्र्कु नलं
आर्त्तिनाळुं अरियामै अकट्रि्र अरिविप्पान् एवन् अप्-
पोर्त्तमुतलै गणपतियै पुकऴ़्न्तु शरणमडैकिन्राम्।

mūrttiyāki talamāki munnīr gangai mutalāna
tīrthamāki arintariyā tirattinālum uyirkku nalam
ārttināḷum ariyāmai akaṭṭri arivippān evan apport-
tamutalai gaṇapatiyai pukazhntu śaraṇamaḍaikinrām.

3. Idarkal muzhutum

I seek refuge at the feet of Ganapati,
the Lord with the single tusk,
the Lord of spiritual attendants,
by whose grace all sorrows get destroyed like cotton in fire,
who makes living beings evolve into angels,
who enables the successful completion of all tasks.

4. Mūrtiyāki talamāki

I pay homage and seek refuge in that primal being,
Ganapati, the Lord of spiritual attendants,
who becomes the idol, the holy place (of pilgrimage) and purifying rivers like the Ganga,
who always does good to living beings, and removes their ignorance.

रागः मोहनं

Raga: Mohanam

5. चेय्युं विनैयिन् मुतल् यावन् चेय्यप्परं अप्पोरुळ् यावन्
ऐयमिन्र उळताकुं अन्त करुमपयन् यावन्
उय्युं विनैयिन् पयन् विळैविन् उट्टुविरुप्पान् एवन् अन्त
पोय्यिल् इरैयै गणपतियै पुकऴ्न्तु शरणमडैंकिन्राम्।

ceyyum vinaiyin mutal yāvan ceyyapparam apporuḷ yāvan
iyaminra uḷatākum anta karumapayan yāvan
uyyum vinaiyin payan viḷaivin uṭṭuviruppān evan anta
poyyiliṛaiyai gaṇapatiyai pukazhntu śaraṇamaḍaikinrām.

रागः मोहनं

Raga: Mohanam

6. वेदं अळन्तुं अरिवरिय विमलन् यावन् वाऴ्त्तुकाय
वेदं मुटिविल् नटं नविलुंविमलन् यावन् विऴक्कुवर्
नादं मुटिविल् वीट्ट्रिरुक्कुम् नातन् एवन् एण् गुणन् एवन् अप्
पोद मुटिविल् गणपतियै पुरिन्तु शरणमडैकिन्राम्।

vedam aḷantum arivariya vimalan yāvan vāzhttukāya
vedam muṭivil naṭam navilum vimalan yāvan vizhakkuvar
nādam muṭivil vīṭṭrirukkum nātan evan eṇ guṇan evan ap
podamuṭivil gaṇapatiyai purintu śaraṇamaḍaikinrām.

5. Ceyyum vinaiyin

I pay homage and seek refuge in that eternal Supreme Being, Ganapati, the Lord of spiritual attendants,
who is the cause of all action,
who makes us do those actions,
who is the cause of creating the results of those actions,
and who makes us experience the results of our actions.

6. Vedam alantum

I seek refuge in that Supreme Being, the embodiment of total bliss, Ganapati, the Lord of spiritual attendants,
who cannot be discerned even by the Vedas,
the flawless One,
who strides the esteemed Upanishads as the pure One,
the Leader who pervades all sound and is seated in the primal *Pranava* sound, *AUM*,
and who has eight qualities.

रागः सुरुट्टि

Raga: Suruṭṭi

7. मण्णिन् ओर् ऐङ्गुणमाकि वतिवान् एवन् नीरिटै नान्काय्
नण्णि अमर्वान एवन तीयिल् मून्राय् नविल्वान् एवन् वळियिन्
एण्णुं इरण्डु गुणमाकि इयल्वान् एवन् वानिडै ओन्राय्
अण्णल् एवन् अग्गणपतियै अन्पिर् शरणमडैकिन्राम्।

maṇṇin or ainguṇamāki vativān evan nīriṭai nānkāi
naṇṇi amarvān evan tīyil mūnrāi navilvān evan vaḷiyin
eṇṇum iraṇḍu guṇamāki iyalvān evan vāniḍai onrāi
aṇṇal evan aggaṇapatiyai anpir śaraṇamaḍaikinrām.

रागः सुरुट्टि

Raga: Suruṭṭi

8. पाश अरिवुं पशु अरिवुं पट्ट्रर्करिय परन् यावन्
पाश अरिवुं पशु अरिवुं पयिलप्पणिक्कुं अवन् यावन् अप्
पाश अरिवुं पशु अरिवुं माट्ट्रिमेलां अरिवान्
देश मुतलै गणपतियै तिकऴु शरणमडैकिन्रान्।

pāśa arivum paśu arivum paṭṭarkariya paran yāvan
pāśa arivum paśu arivum payilappaṇikkum avan yāv-an ap
pāśa arivum paśu arivum māṭṭrimelām arivān
deśa mutalai gaṇapatiyai tikazhu śaraṇamaḍaikinrām.

7. Mannin or aingunamāki

I lovingly seek refuge in that Ganapati, the Lord of spiritual attendants,
who shines as the five qualities of the earth (sound, touch, form, taste, smell),
as four qualities of water (sound, touch, form and taste),
as the three qualities of fire (sound, touch, form),
as the two qualities of wind (sound and touch),
as the one quality of ether (sky): sound.

8. Pāśa arivum paśu aṛivum

I seek total refuge in that primal being, Ganapati,
the Lord of spiritual attendants,
the Supreme Being, who cannot be discerned by knowledge, so long as the soul is bound by bondage (of the three evils: ego, karma and delusion),
the Lord who makes us realise about soul and its bondage,
and can remove the bondage from the soul.

HYMNS TO GAṆEŚA BY VEDA VYASA

	Hymn	*Raga*
1.	Gaṇeśashṭakam from Gaṇeśa Purāṇa	Ragamalika*
2.	Siddhivināyaka stotram from Mudgala Purāṇa	Ragamalika*
3.	Sankata nāśana ganapati stotram from Nārada Purāṇa	Ragamalika*
4.	Gaṇeśashṭakam from Padma Purāṇa	Ragamalika*

*Hamsadhwani, Mālahari, Kalyāṇavasantam, Kuntālavarāḷi, Yamunā Kalyāṇi, Sindhubhairavi, Hindolam, Madhyamāvati.

VEDA VYASA

VEDA VYASA (13th Century B.C.)

Veda Vyasa, the author of the epic *Mahābhārata* and *Bhāgavata* and other Puranas, was the son of Sage Parāśara and the fisherwoman Satyavati.

The late sage of Kanchi, Paramāchārya, said of Vyasa: "There is no means of approach to the Supreme, which does not find a place in one or other works of Vyasa. Bhagavan Vyasa is a *Mārgadarśi* (Pathfinder) without an equal in any country or age."

Veda Vyasa was a great Yogi, great *Jnāni,* great mystical devotee and lover of God, apart from being a great poet.

श्रीगणेशाष्टकम् (गणेशपुराणे अन्तर्गतं)

रागः हंसध्वनि　　　　Raga: Hamsadhwani

1. यतोऽनन्तशक्तेरनन्ताश्च जीवाः
यतो निर्गुणादप्रमेया गुणास्ते।
यतो भाति सर्वं त्रिधाभेदभिन्नम्
सदा तं गणेशं नमामो भजामः।।

yatoanantaśakteranantāśca jīvāḥ
yato nirguṇādaprameyā guṇāste
yato bhāti sarvam tridhābhedabhinnam
sadā tam gaṇeśam namāmo bhajāmaḥ.

रागः मालहरि　　　　Raga: Mālahari

2. यतश्चाविरासीत् जगत्सर्वमेतत्
तथाऽब्जासनो विश्वगो विश्वगोप्ता।
तथेन्द्रादयो देवसंघा मनुष्याः
सदा तं गणेशं नमामो भजामः।।

yataścāvirāsīt jagatsarvametat
tathābjāsano viśvago viśvagoptā
tathendrādayo devasanghā manushyāḥ
sadā tam gaṇeśam namāmo bhajāmaḥ.

Gaṇeśāshṭakam from Gaṇeśa Purāṇa

1. We ever prostrate and meditate on that Gaṇeśa,
   from whose limitless power have been born myriad lives,
   who is attributeless, yet immeasurable attributes have risen out of Him,
   because of whom, everything shines divided into triads.*

2. We ever prostrate and meditate on that Gaṇeśa,
   from whom the entire universe has been born,
   from whom have manifested the Creator, Preserver and Destroyer, as also the celestials headed by Indra and all mankind.

*The various triads are:

1. The three states: waking, dream and deep sleep.
2. The three periods of time: past, present, future.
3. The three bodies: gross, subtle, causal.
4. The trinity: Creator, Preserver, Destroyer.
5. The three qualities: sattva, rajas, tamas.
6. The three worlds: earth, heaven, netherworld.
7. Three types of activity: creation, maintenance, destruction.

रागः कल्याणवसन्तं | Raga: Kalyāṇavasantam

3. यतो वह्निमान् भवो भूर्जलं च
यतः सागराश्चन्द्रमा व्योम वायुः।
यतः स्थावरा जंगमा वृक्षसंघाः
सदा तं गणेशं नमामो भजामः।।

yato vahnimān bhavo bhūrjalam ca
yataḥ sāgarāścandramā vyoma vāyuḥ
yataḥ sthāvarā jangamā vṛkṣasanghāḥ
sadā tam gaṇeśam namāmo bhajāmaḥ.

रागः कुंतालवराळि | Raga: Kuntālavarāḷi

4. यतो दानवाः किन्नरा यक्षसंघाः
यतश्चारणाः वारणाः श्वापदाश्च।
यतः पक्षिकीटाः यतो वीरुधश्च
सदा तं गणेशं नमामो भजामः।।

yato dānavāḥ kinnarā yakṣasamghāḥ
yataścāraṇāḥ vāraṇāḥ śvāpadāśca
yataḥ pakṣikīṭāḥ yato vīrudhaśca
sadā tam gaṇeśam namāmo bhajāmaḥ.

3. We ever prostrate and meditate on that Ganesa, from whom have been born fire, sun, all creation, the earth, water, the oceans, the moon, ether, wind, all that moves and does not move and multitudes of trees.

4. We ever prostrate and meditate on that Ganesa, from whom have been born demons, *kinnaras*, *yakshas*, *cāraṇas*, elephants, animals, birds, worms, and creepers.

Kinnaras are mythical beings with heads of horses and human bodies. *Yakshas* are spirits or ghosts, demigods in nature.

Cāraṇas are celestial singers.

रागः यमुनाकल्याणि — Raga: Yamunākalyāṇi

5. यतो बुद्धिरज्ञाननाशो मुमुक्षोः
यतः संपदो भक्तसन्तोषिकाः स्युः।
यतो विघ्ननाशो यतः कार्यसिद्धिः
सदा तं गणेशं नमामो भजामः।।

yato buddhirajnānanāśo mumukṣoḥ
yataḥ sampado bhaktasantoṣikāḥ syuḥ
yato vighnanāśo yataḥ kāryasiddhiḥ
sadā tam gaṇeśam namāmo bhajāmaḥ.

रागः सिंधुभैरवि — Raga: Sindhubhairavi

6. यतः पुत्रसंपद्यतो वांछितार्थो
यतोऽभक्तविघ्नास्तथाऽनेकरूपाः।
यतः शोकमोहौ यतः काम एव
सदा तं गणेशं नमामो भजामः।।

yataḥ putrasampadyato vānchitārtho
yato abhaktavighnāstathānekarūpāḥ
yataḥ śokamohau yataḥ kāma eva
sadā tam gaṇeśam namāmo bhajāmaḥ.

5. We ever prostrate and meditate on that Ganesa,
because of whom ignorance of those desiring liberation gets destroyed,
devotees attain bliss and prosperity,
obstacles get removed
and tasks are accomplished successfully.

6. We ever prostrate and meditate on that Ganesa,
from whom are attained the blessing of progeny and all other forms of goals desired,
and all kinds of obstacles, sorrow, delusion, attachment etc. result for those who are not devoted to Him.

रागः हिन्दोलं Raga: Hindolam

7. यतोनन्तशक्तिः स शेषो बभूव
धराधारणेऽनेकरूपे च शक्तः।
यतोनेकधा सर्वलोका हि नाना
सदा तं गणेशं नमामो भजामः।।

yatonantaśaktiḥ sa śeṣo babhūva
dharādhāraṇeanekarūpe ca śaktaḥ
yatonekadhā sarvalokā hi nānā
sadā tam gaṇeśam namāmo bhajāmaḥ.

रागः मध्यमावति Raga: Madhyamāvati

8. यतो वेदवाचो विकण्ठा मनोभिः
सदा नेति नेतीति यत्ता गृणन्ति।
परब्रह्मरूपं चिदानन्दभूतम्
सदा तं गणेशं नमामो भजामः।।

yato vedavāco vikaṇṭha manobhiḥ
sadā neti netīti yattā gṛṇanti
parabrahmarūpam cidānanda bhūtam
sadā tam gaṇeśam namāmo bhajāmaḥ.

7. We ever prostrate and meditate on that Ganesa,
from whom was born *Ādi Sesha* with enormous power
and became strong enough to bear the worlds,
and from whom myriad worlds have been created.

8. We ever prostrate and meditate on that *Ganesa,*
from whom have been born the unimaginable Vedic words, which proclaim that all that is perceptible is not the ultimate reality
and who is the embodiment of the Supreme God,
who is consciousness-bliss.

सिद्धिविनायक स्तोत्रम (मुद्गल पुराणे अन्तर्गतं)

रागः हंसध्वनि Raga: Hamsadhwani

1. विघ्नेश विघ्नचयखण्डन नामधेय
श्रीशंकरात्मज सुराधिपवन्द्यपाद।
दुर्गामहाव्रतफलाखिलमङ्गलात्मन्
विघ्नं ममापहर सिद्धिविनायक त्वम्।।

vighneśa vighnacayakhaṇḍana nāmadheya
śrī śamkarātmaja surādhipavandyapāda
durgāmahāvrataphalākhilamangalātman
vighnam mamāpahara siddhivināyaka tvam.

रागः मालहरि Raga: Mālahari

2. सत्पद्मराग मणिवर्णशरीरकान्तिः
श्रीसिद्धिबुद्धिपरिचर्चितकुङ्कुम श्रीः।
दक्षस्तने वलयितातिमानोज्ञशुण्डो
विघ्नं ममापहर सिद्धिविनायक त्वम्।।

satpadmarāgamaṇivarṇaśarīrakāntiḥ
śrīsiddhibuddhiparicarcitakumkumaśrīḥ
dakṣastane valayitātimanojnaśuṇḍo
vighnam mamāpahara siddhivināyaka tvam.

Siddhivinayaka Stotram from Mudgala Purana

1. O Lord of obstacles,
   who are reputed as the destroyer of clusters of obstacles!
   O son of *Śiva*, the Creator of bliss!
   O Lord, whose feet are worshipped by *Indra*, the Chief of celestials!
   O granter of results for the great ritual* in honour of Durga, the Divine Mother!
   O embodiment of total auspiciousness!
   O Lord who have no leader above you and are the embodiment of success!
   Take away my obstacles!

2. O Lord, whose body is beautiful like the best coral and radiant with the vermilion marks of Siddhi and Buddhi (Success and knowledge, your deemed spouses)!
   Your trunk is so very attractive, curling against your upright chest!
   Take away my obstacles! O *Siddhi Vināyaka*!
   You who have no leader above you and are the embodiment of success!

*The reference here is to the nine-day *Navaratri Puja* (also known as Dussehra and Durga Puja) commencing on the new moon (Mahalaya Amavasya) in September-October, every year and extending upto Vijaya Dasami day (tenth digit after new moon), when the Divine Mother is worshipped specially in all parts of India.

रागः कल्याणवसन्तं — Raga: Kalyāṇavasantam

3. पाशाङ्कुशाब्जपरशूंश्च दधच्चतुर्भि
दोर्भिश्च शोणकूसुमस्रगुमाङ्गजातः।
सिन्दूरशोभित ललाटविधुप्रकाशो
विघ्नं ममापहर सिद्धिविनायक त्वम्।।

pāśānkuśābjaparasūnśca dadhaccaturbhir
dobhiśca śoṇakusumasragumāngajātaḥ
sindūraśobhita lalāṭavidhuprakāśo
vighnam mamāpahara siddhivināyaka tvam.

रागः कुन्तालवराळि — Raga: Kuntālavarāḷi

4. कार्येषु विघ्नचयभीतविरिञ्चिमुख्यैः
सम्पूजितः सुरवरैरपि मोदकाद्यैः।
सर्वेषु च प्रथममेव सुरेषु पूज्यो
विघ्नं ममापहर सिद्धिविनायक त्वम्।।

kāryeṣu vighnacayabhītavirincimukhyaiḥ
sampūjitaḥ suravarairapi modakādyaiḥ
sarveṣu ca prathamameva sureṣu pūjyo
vighnam mamāpahara siddhivināyaka tvam.

3. O Lord who hold the noose, goad, lotus and the axe in your four hands!
You wear a garland of red flowers!
You are born of *Uma,* the Divine Mother!
You wear a vermilion mark on your forehead and the crescent moon shines in your crest!
O *Siddhivinayaka*!
You who have no leader above you and are the embodiment of success!
Take away my obstacles!

4. Fearing impending obstacles in their tasks, Brahma, the creator and other celestials worshipped you well with eats like rice cakes!
Of all angels, you are worshipped first!
O Siddhi Vinayaka!
You who have no leader above you and are the embodiment of success!
Take away my obstacles!

रागः यमुनाकल्याणि | Raga: Yamunākalyāṇi

5. शीघ्राञ्जनस्खलनतुङ्गरवोर्ध्वकण्ठ
स्थूलेन्दुरुद्रगणहासितदेवसंघः।
शूर्पश्रुतिश्च पृथुवर्तुलतुङ्गतुन्दो
विघ्नं ममापहर सिद्धिविनायक त्वम्।।

śīghrānjanaskhalanatungaravordhvakaṇṭha
sthūlendurudragaṇahāsitadevasanghaḥ
śūrpaśrutiśca pṛthuvartulatungatundo
vighnam mamāpahara siddhivināyaka tvam.

रागः सिंधुभैरवि | Raga: Sindhubhairavi

6. यज्ञोपवीतपदलम्भितनागराजो
मासादिपुण्यद दृशीकृत ऋक्षराजः।
भक्ताभयप्रद दयालय विघ्नराज
विघ्नं ममापहर सिद्धिविनायक त्वम्।।

yajnopavītapadalambhitanāgarājo
māsādipuṇyadadṛśīkṛta rikṣarājaḥ
bhaktābhayaprada dayālaya vighnarāja
vighnam mamāpahara siddhivināyaka tvam.

5. Your neck can move very fast and can produce loud noise!
You are moon-crested!
You make the attendants of Siva (your father) and the multitudes of celestials laugh by your pranks!
Your ears resemble the winnowing mat!
You have a big and round belly!
O Siddhi Vinayaka!
You who have no leader above you and are the embodiment of success!
Take away my obstacles!

6. You wear the serpent king as your sacred thread!
You bestow boons on those who worship you on the first of months and full moons!
You give freedom from fear to your devotees!
You are the abode of compassion!
O Lord of obstacles! O *Siddhi Vinayaka*!
You who have no leader above you and are the embodiment of success!
Take away my obstacles!

रागः हिन्दोलं

Raga: Hindolam

7. सद्रत्न सारततिराजितसत्किरीटः
कौसुम्भ चारुवसनद्वय ऊर्जित श्रीः।
सर्वत्र मङ्गलकरस्मरणप्रतापो
विघ्नं ममापहर सिद्धविनायक त्वम्।।

sadratnasāratatirājitasatkirīṭaḥ
kausumbhacāruvasanadvaya ūrjita śrīḥ
sarvatra mangalakarasmaraṇapratāpo
vighnam mamāpahara siddhivināyaka tvam.

रागः मध्यमावति

Raga: Madhyamāvati

8. देवान्तकाद्यसुर भीतसुरार्तिहर्ता
विज्ञानबोधवरेण तमोऽपहर्ता।
आनन्दित त्रिभुवनेश कुमारबन्धो
विघ्नं ममापहर सिद्धिविनायक त्वम्।।

devāntakādyasura bhītasurārtihartā
vijnānabodhavareṇa tamopahartā
ānanditatribhuvaneśa kumārabandho
vighnam mamāpahara siddhivināyaka tvam.

7. You wear a crown on your head, studded with the choicest jewels!
You wear two very beautiful silken garments!
When remembered, You create auspiciousness everywhere!
O *Siddhi Vinayaka*!
You who have no leader above you, and are the embodiment of success!
Take away my obstacles!

8. You removed the distress of the celestials, harassed by demons like *Devānthaka*!
You destroy the darkness of ignorance, by the boon of divine knowledge!
You rendered happy Kumara (Subramania) and the Lord of the three worlds!
O *Siddhi Vinayaka*!
You who have no leader above you, and are the embodiment of success!
Take away my obstacles!

संकटनाश गणपति स्तोत्रम् (नारद पुराणे)

रागः हंसध्वनि — Raga: Hamsadhwani

1. प्रणम्य शिरसा देवं गौरीपुत्रं विनायकं
भक्तवासं स्मरेत् नित्यं आयुः कामार्थसिद्धये।।

paraṇamya śirasā devam gaurīputram vināyakam
bhaktavāsam smaret nityam āyuḥ
kāmārthasiddhaye.

रागः मालहरि — Raga: Mālahari

2. प्रथमं वक्रतुण्डं च एकदन्तं द्वितीयकं
तृतीयं कृष्णपिङ्गाक्षं गजवक्त्रं चतुर्थकं।।

prathamam vakratuṇḍam ca ekadantam
dvitīyakam
tṛtīyam krisṇapingākṣam gajavaktram caturthakam.

रागः कल्याणवसन्तं — Raga: Kalyāṇavasantam

3. लम्बोदरं पञ्चमं च षष्ठं विकटं एव च
सप्तमं विघ्नराजं च धूम्रवर्णं तथाष्ठमम्।।

lambodaram pancamam ca ṣaṣṭham vikaṭam eva ca
saptamam vighnarājam ca dhumravarṇam
tathāṣṭhamam.

Sankaṭanāśa Gaṇapati Stotram (From the Narada Purana)

1. Prostrating head down, one should daily meditate on the Lord, who is the son of the fair goddess, who has no master above Him, who resides in his devotees, in order to attain a long life and get the fulfilment of desires.

2. (Meditate on Him):
First, as the One with the curving trunk,
Second, as the One with one tusk,
Third, as the One with dark brown eyes,
Fourth, as the elephant-faced One!

3. Fifth, as the big bellied One,
Sixth, as the huge One,
Seventh, as the Lord of obstacles,
Eighth, as the smoke-hued One!

रागः कुन्तालवराळि — Raga: Kuntālavarāḷi

4. नवमं फालचन्द्रं च दशमं तु विनायकं
एकादशं गणपतिं द्वादशं तु गजाननम्।

navamam phālacandram ca daśamam tu vināyakam
ekādaśam gaṇapatim dvādaśam tu gajānanam.

रागः यमुनाकल्याणि — Raga: Yamunākalyāṇi

5. द्वादशैतानि नामानि त्रिसन्ध्यां यः पठेत् नरः
न च विघ्नभयं तस्य सर्वसिद्धिकरं परम्।

dvādaśaitāni nāmāni trisandhyām yaḥ paṭhet naraḥ
na ca vighnabhayam tasya sarvasiddhikaram param.

रागः सिन्धुभैरवि — Raga: Sindhubhairavi

6. विद्यार्थी लभते विद्यां धनार्थी लभते धनं
पुत्रार्थी लभते पुत्रं मोक्षार्थी लभते गतिम्।

vidyārthī labhate vidyām dhanārthī labhate dhanam
putrārthī labhate putram mokṣārthī labhate gatim.

4. Ninth, as the One who wears the moon on the forehead,
Tenth, as the One who has no lord above him,
Eleventh, as the Lord of spiritual attendants,
Twelfth, as the elephant-faced One!

5. The person who recites these twelve names at dawn, noon and dusk, has no fear of obstacles and he achieves everything!

6. The seeker after learning gets learning,
the seeker of wealth gets wealth,
one who desires children gets children,
and one who desires liberation attains liberation.

रागः हिन्दोलं Raga: Hindolam

7. जपेत् गणपति स्तोत्रं षड्भिः मासैः फलं लभेत्
संवत्सरेण सिद्धिं च लभते नात्र संशयः।

japet gaṇapati stotram ṣadbhiḥ māsaiḥ phalam labhet
samvatsareṇa siddhim ca labhate nātra samśayaḥ.

रागः मध्यमावति Raga: Madhyamāvati

8. अष्टानां ब्राह्मणानां च लिखित्वा यः समर्पयेत्
तस्य विद्या भवेत् सद्यो गणेशस्य प्रसादत्वात्।

aṣṭānām brāhmaṇānām ca likhitvā yaḥ samarpayet
tasya vidyā bhavet sadyo gaṇeśasya prasādatvāt.

इति श्री नारदपुराणे संकटनाशनं नाम गणपतिस्तोत्रं संपूर्णम्।

iti śrī nāradapurāṇe sankaṭanāśanam nāma gaṇapatistotram sampūrṇam.

7. If this prayer of Ganesa is recited for six months, results are achieved,
In a year supernatural powers are attained,
There is no doubt about this.

8. If the prayer is written and given to eight seekers of God, one immediately becomes the master of all learning, due to the grace of Ganesa.

Thus is complete the prayer to Lord Ganesa, which occurs in the Narada Purana and is the destroyer of all sorrow.

पद्मपुराणे अन्तर्गतं गणेशाष्टकम्

रागः हंसध्वनि Raga: Hamsadhwani

1. गणपतिपरिवारं चारुकेयूरहारं
गिरिधरवरसारं योगिनीचक्रचारम्।
भवभयपरिहारं दुःखदारिद्र्यदूरं
गणपतिमभिवन्दे वक्रतुण्डावतारम्।।

ganapati parivāraṁ cārukeyūrahāram
giridhara varasāram yoginīcakracāram
bhava bhaya parihāram duḥkhadāridryadūram
gaṇapatimabhivande vakratuṇḍāvatāram.

रागः मालहरि Raga: Mālahari

2. अखिल मलविनाशं पाणिना हस्तपाशं
कनकगिरि निकाशं सूर्य कोटि प्रकाशं।
भज भवगिरिनाशं मालतीतीरवासं
गणपतिमभिवन्दे मानसे राजहंसं।।

akhilamalavināśam pāṇinā hastapāśam
kanakagirinikāśam sūryakoṭiprakāśam
bhaja bhavagirināśam mālatītīravāsam
gaṇapatimabhivande mānase rājahamsam.

Gaṇeśāṣṭakam
(From Padmapurana)

1. I bow to Ganesa, the lord of *Gaṇas,**
who is accompanied by a retinue, wears a golden necklace,
who gave a boon to Krishna, the holder of the mountain,
who walks the Yogini cakra,
who destroys the fear of *samsara,*
who removes sorrow and penury,
and has manifested as the elephant-faced One,
with the curved trunk.

2. I bow to Ganesa, the lord of *Ganas,*
who destroys all sins, holds the noose in his hand,
who resides in the golden mountain,
has the effulgence of a million suns,
who destroys the mountain of samsaric woes,
who resides on the banks of the Malati river,
and who is like the royal swan in the lake of my mind.

**Gaṇas* are spiritual (Siva) attendants.

रागः कल्याणवसन्तं Raga: Kalyāṇavasantam

3. विविध मणिमयूखैः शोभमानं विदुरैः
कनक रचितचित्रं कण्ठदेशे विचित्रं।
दधति विमलहारं सर्वदा यत्नसारं
गणपतिमभिवन्दे वक्रतुण्डावतारं।।

vividhamaṇimayūkhaiḥ śobhamānam viduraiḥ
kanakaracitacitram kaṇṭhadeśe vicitram
dadhati vimalahāram sarvadā yatnasāram
gaṇapatimabhivande vakratuṇḍāvatāram.

रागः कुन्तालवराळि Raga: Kuntālavarāḷi

4. दुरितगजममन्दं वारुणीं चैव वेदं
विदितमखिलनादं नृत्यमानन्दकन्दं।
दधति शशिसुवक्त्रं चांकुशं यो विशेषं
गणपतिमभिवन्दे सर्वदानन्दकन्दं।।

duritagajamamandam vāruṇīm caiva vedam
viditamakhilanādam nṛtyamānandakandam
dadhatiśaśisuvaktram cānkuśam yo viśeṣam
gaṇapatimabhivande sarvadānandakandam.

3. I bow to Ganeśa, the lord of *Ganas,*
who shines with the rays emanating from diverse gems,
who wears round his neck gold ornaments,
wears a stainless garland,
is always inclined to ceaseless effort, and
who has manifested as the elephant-faced One,
with the curved trunk.

4. I bow to Ganesa, the Lord of *Ganas,*
who controls the elephant of sorrow,
who is the embodiment of the Vedas,
who knows all the sounds, and dances in joyous bliss,
wears the moon and holds the spear,
and who is always the treasurehouse of bliss.

रागः यमुनाकल्याणि

Raga: Yamunākalyāṇi

5. त्रिनयनयुतभाले शोभमाने विशाले
मुकुटमणि सुढाले मौक्तिकानां च जाले।
धवलकुसुममाले यस्य शीर्ष्णः सताले
गणपतिमभिवन्दे सर्वदा चक्रपाणिम्।।

trinayanayutabhāle śobhamāne viśāle
mukuṭamaṇisuḍhāle mauktikānām ca jāle
dhavalakusumamāle yasya śīṣrṇah satāle
gaṇapatimabhivande sarvadā cakrapāṇim.

रागः सिन्धुभैरवि

Raga: Sindhubhairavi

6. वपुषि महति रूपं पीठमादौ सुदीपं
तदुपरि रसकोणं यस्य चोर्ध्वं त्रिकोणं।
गजमितदलपद्मं संस्थितं चारुछद्मं
गणपतिमभिवन्दे कल्पवृक्षस्य वृन्दे।।

vapuṣi mahati rūpam pīṭhamādau sudīpam
tadupari rasakoṇam yasya cordhwam trikoṇam
gajamitadalapadmam samsthitam cāruchadmam
gaṇapatimabhivande kalpavṛkṣasya vṛṇde.

5. I bow to Ganesa, the Lord of Ganas (spiritual attendants),
whose head has three eyes on the forehead,
who has a crown studded with gems and rolls of pearls,
who wears a garland of white flowers, and
who always holds the discus.

6. I bow to Ganesa, the Lord of Ganas,
among the clusters of *Kalpa* tree,
whose form is gigantic in body,
who has a seat in front, lit by a lamp,
and above it is a triangle and above it another triangle,
who is established in the beautiful six-petalled lotus (*Muladhara*).

राग: हिन्दोलं Raga: Hindolam

7. वरदविशदशस्तं दक्षिणं यस्य हस्तं
सदयमभयदं तं चिन्तये चित्तसंस्थं।
शबलकुटिलशुण्डं चैकतुण्डं द्वितुण्डं
गणपतिमभिवन्दे सर्वदा वक्रतुण्डं।।

varadaviśadaśastam dakṣiṇam yasya hastam
sadayamabhayadam tam cintaye cittasamstham
śabalakuṭilaśuṇḍam caikatuṇḍam dvituṇḍam
gaṇapatimabhivande sarvadā vakratuṇḍam.

राग: मध्यमावति Raga: Madhyamāvati

8. कल्पद्रुमाधः स्थित कामधेनुं
चिन्तामणिं दक्षिणपाणिशुण्डं।
बिभ्राणमत्यद्भुत चित्ररूपं
यः पूजयेत्तस्य समस्त सिद्धिः।।

kalpadrumādhasthitakāmadhenum
cintāmaṇim dakṣiṇapāṇiśuṇḍam
bibhrāṇamatyadbhutacitrarūpam
yaḥ pūjayettasya samastasiddhiḥ.

व्यासाष्टकमिदं पुण्यं गणेश स्तवनं नृणां
पठतां दुःखनाशाय विद्यां सश्रियमश्नुते।।

vyāsāṣṭakamidam puṇyam gaṇeśastavanam nṛṇām
paṭhatām dukhanāśāya vidyām saśriyamaśnute.

7. I bow to Ganesa, the Lord of Ganas,
whose right hand grants abundant boons,
who compassionately gives freedom from fear,
I ever think of him as located in my heart,
with the curved trunk.

8. He who worships the radiant wondrous form (of Ganesa),
who is like the *Kamadhenu* and *Cintamani* located under the *Kalpa* tree,*
holding his trunk in his right hand, attains everything.

Those who read this eight-versed hymn composed by Vyasa, in honour of Ganesa, attains blessedness and learning and all sorrows are destroyed.

**Kāmadhenu*, the celestial cow, *Cintamani* stone and the *Kalpa* tree are three wish-granting objects in Hindu mythology.

HYMN TO GAṆEŚA BY TIRUMULAR

Hymn	*Raga*
1. Aintukaraṇe	Nāṭa

TIRUMULAR

TIRUMULAR (3rd Century A.D.–5th Century A.D.)

Tirumular is considered the foremost among the mystic saints of Tamil Nadu.

Tirumular's *magnum opus* is *Tirumantiram*, a work comprising 3000 stanzas.

He belonged to the Saiva Siddhanta school of philosophy.

His main teaching was: "Love is God and God is one and so is mankind."

The songs of Tirumular in praise of Lord Siva will be presented in Volume Eight of the Sacred Songs of India.

The hymn to Ganesa included in this volume is a rare composition of Tirumular.

रागः नाट Raga: Nāṭa

ऐन्दु करत्तनै आनैमुखत्तनै
इन्दिन् इळंपिरै पोलुं एयिट्ट्रनै
नन्दि मकन् तन्नै ज्ञान क्कोळुन्तिनैप्
पुन्दियिल् वैत्तटि पोट्ट्रुकिन्रेने।

eindu karattanai ānai mukhattanai
indin iḷampirai polum eyiṭṭranai
nandimakan tannai jnāna kkozhuntinaip
pundiyil vaittaṭi poṭṭrukinrene.

Aintukarattanai

I worship, treasuring in my heart,
the five-armed Lord
the Elephant-faced One!
who rises like the rays of the rising moon
Son of Siva (whose bodyguard is Nandi),
the embodiment of knowledge.

HYMN TO GAṆEŚA BY AVVAIYAR

	Hymn	*Raga*
1.	Vinayakar Akaval	Ragamalika

AVVAIYAR

AVVAIYAR (7th Century A.D.)

Avvaiyar, "the grandmother of Tamil literature", as she is affectionately called, was one of the greatest singer saints of ancient India.

Myth and legend have covered in mist the biographical details of Avvaiyar's life.

Many believe that there was more than one Avvaiyar. She could have been born any time during the period 3rd century B.C. to 7th century A.D.

There is a statue of Avvaiyar on the Marina beach in Chennai (India) under which her birth date is mentioned as 1st century B.C.

But the Avvaiyar who has authored *Vināyakar Akaval*, included in this volume, was more probably a contemporary of the Saivite saint Sundarar, who probably lived in the 7th or 8th century A.D.

Avvaiyar was a great devotee of Lord Gaṇeśa and is considered the pioneer saint who propagated worship of Gaṇeśa in South India.

Avvaiyar's *Vināyakar Akaval* is a veritable treasurehouse of devotion through the Yogic path.

To present this immortal jewel of a devotional song in this compendium of hymns to Gaṇeśa is a proud privilege.

विनायक अकवल्

रागः नाटै Raga: Nāṭai

1. शीत कळभच्चेन्तामरै पूं
पाद चिलम्पु पल इशै पाड

śītakaḷabhaccentāmarai pūm
pādacilampu pala iśai pāḍa

2. पोन् अरैज्ञाणुं पून्तुकिल् आडैयुं
वण्ण मरुङ्किल् वळर्न्तु अऴकु नरिप्प

pon arai jnāṇum pūntukil āḍaiyum
vaṇṇa marunkil vaḷarntu azhaku naṛippa

3. प्पेऴै वयिरुं पेरम्पार कोटुं
वेऴ मुखमुं विळङ्कु चिन्तूरमुं

ppezhai vayirum perampāra koṭum
vezhamukhamum viḷankucintūramum

4. अञ्चु करमुं अङ्कुशपाशमुं
नेञ्चिल् कुटि कोण्ड नील मेनियुं

ancu karamum ankuśapāśamum
nencil kuṭi koṇḍa nīlameniyum

रागः हंसध्वनि Raga: Hamsadhwani

5. नान्र वायुं नालिरु पुयमुं
मून्रु कण्णुं मुमदचुवटुं

nānra vāyum nāliru puyamum
mūnru kaṇṇum mumadacuvaṭum

Vinayakar Akaval of Avvaiyar

1. Your feet are like the red lotus, cool and fragrant!
The anklets on them produce myriad musical sounds!

2. The gold chain and the beautiful new cloth on the waist are radiant like the rays of the sun!

3. You have a big belly, a powerful tusk and an elephant face!
The vermilion mark on that face shines!

4. You have five hands, the goad and the noose (in your hands)!
Your body is blue. You ever reside in the heart!

5. Your mouth is a hanging trunk! You have four big shoulders!
You have three eyes and three stains (of ichor)!

6. इरण्डु चेवियुं इलङ्कु पोन्मुटियुं
तिरण्ड मुप्पुरिनूल् तिकऴोळिमार्पुं

irandu ceviyum ilanku ponmuṭiyum
tiraṇḍa muppurinūl tikazhoḷimārpum

7. चोर्पदं कटन्त तुरिय मेय्ज्ञान
अर्भुतं निन्र कर्पक कळिरे

corpadam kaṭanta turiya meyjjnāna
arbhutam ninra karpaka kaḷire

8. मुप्पऴं नुकरुं मूषिक वाहन
इप्पोऴुतु एन्तै आट्कोळ्वेण्टित्

muppazham nukarum mūṣikavāhana
ippozhutu entai āṭkoḷveṇṭit

रागः मोहनं Raga: Mohanam

9. तायाय् एनक्कु तान् एऴुन्तरुळि
मायाप्पिरवि मयक्कं अरुत्तु

tāyāy enakku tān ezhuntaruḷi
māyāppiṛavi mayakkam aruttu

6. You have two ears and a golden crown!
Your chest is adorned by a three-stringed sacred thread!

7. You are in that transcendental state of grace which is beyond words! O Lord in the form of the male elephant!
You are like the Kalpaka tree, granting all wishes!

8. You eat three fruits (the mango, the jackfruit and banana)!
O Lord who ride a mouse!
Come and enslave me this moment!*

9. Be my mother, appear on your own before me and bless me!
And cut asunder this delusion of recurring birth!

---

*The myth about Ganesa riding a mouse is like this: The demon Gajamukha attacked assuming the form of a giant rat. Ganesa reduced him to a tiny mouse and graciously agreed to ride him, when the demon surrendered.

10. तिरुन्तिय मुतल् ऐन्तेऴुत्तुं तेळिवाय्
प्पोरुन्तवे वन्तेन् उळन्तनिल् पुकुन्तु

tiruntiya mutal eintezhuttum teḷivāy
pporuntave vanten uḷantanil pukuntu

11. गुरु वटिवाकि क्कुवलयं तन्निल्
तिरुवटि वैत्तु त्तिरमितु पोरुळेन

guru vaṭivāki kkuvalayam tannil
tiruvaṭi vaittu ttiramitu poruḷena

12. वाटा वकैतान् मकिऴ्न्तेनक्करुळिक्
कोटायुधत्ताल् कोटुविनै कऴैन्ते

vāṭāvakaitān makizhntenakkaruḷik
koṭāyudhattāl koṭuvinai kazhainte

राग: कांबोजि

Raga: Kāmboji

13. उवट्टा उपदेशं पुकट्टि एन् चेवियिल्
तेविट्टात ज्ञान त्तेळिवेयुं काट्टि

uvaṭṭā upadeśam pukaṭṭi en ceviyil
teviṭṭāta jnānatteḷiveyum kāṭṭi

14. ऐम्पुलन् तन्नै अटक्कुं उपायं
इन्पुरु करुणैयिन् इनितेनक्कु अरुळिक्

eimpulan tannai aṭakkum upāyam
inpuru karuṇaiyin initenakku aruḷik

10. Enter my heart in the appropriate way so that the meaning of the five-lettered mantra (*Namah śivāya*) is clear to me!

11. Place your holy feet on this earth, in the form of the Teacher, who bestows enlightenment!

12. Grant me sorrowless bliss and destroy my sins with the axe of your benevolent eye!

13. Render unto my ears the words of wisdom that are sweet and never satiate!

14. Teach me the way to control the five senses and the path to blissful beatitude!

15. करुविकळ् ओटुङ्कुं करुत्तिनै अरिवित्तु
इरुविनै तन्नै अरुत्तु इरुळ् कटिन्तु

karuvikaḷ oṭunkum karuttinai arivittu
iruvinai tannai aruttu iruḷ kaṭintu

रागः तोडि — Raga: Toḍi

16. तलं ओरु नान्कुं तन्न्तेनक्करुळि
मलं ओरु मून्रिन् मयक्कं अरुत्ते

talam oru nānkum tanntenakkaruḷi
malam oru mūnrin mayakkam arutte

17. ओन्पतु वायिल् ओरु मन्तिरत्ताल्
ऐम्पुल क्कतवै अटैप्पतुं काट्टि

onpatu vāyil oru mantirattāl
eimpula kkatavai aṭaippatum kāṭṭi

18. आरातारात्तु अङ्कुश निलैयुं
पेरा निरुत्ति पेच्चुरै अरुत्ते

ārātārāttu ankuśa nilaiyum
perā nirutti peccurai arutte

रागः कल्याणवसन्तं — Raga: Kalyāṇavasantam

19. इटै पिङ्गलयिन् एऴुत्तरिवित्तुक्
कटैयिल् सुऴुमुनै कपालमुं काट्टि

iṭai pingalayin ezhuttarivittuk
kaṭaiyil suzhumunai kapālamum kātti

15. Teach me that knowledge which will wean my senses and the mind from worldly entanglements, and destroy the darkness of the ego and rid me of both vice and virtue!

16. Grant me the four states (the waking, dream, sleeping and the transcendent *(Turiya)* state)
and remove the delusion arising out of the three sins (arrogance, attachment and illusion)!

17. With the peerless Pranava Mantra: AUM, kindly show the way to close the nine openings and the five doors of this body!

18. Grant me the state that transcends the six cakras (Muladhara, Swadhistana, Manipuraka, Anahata, Visuddhi and Ajna), and the silence that puts an end to my prattle!

19. Teach me the way to raise the Kundalini through *Ida, Pingala* and *Sushumna* to *Sahasrara*!

20. मून्रु मण्डलत्तिन् मुट्टिय तूणिन्
नान्रु एऴुपाम्पिन् नाविल् उणर्त्तिक्

mūnrumaṇḍalattin muṭṭiya tūṇin
nānru ezhupāmpin nāvil uṇarttik

21. कुण्डलि अतनिल् कूटिय अचपै
विण्डेऴु मन्तिरं वेळिप्पड उरैत्तु

kuṇḍali atanil kūṭiya acapai
viṇḍezhu mantiram veḷippaḍa uraittu

रागः यमुनाकल्याणि — Raga: Yamunākalyāṇi

22. मूलाधारत्तिन् मुण्डेऴु कनलैक्
कालाल् एऴुप्पुं करुत्तरिवित्ते

mūlādhārattin muṇḍezhu kanalaik
kālāl ezhuppum karuttarivitte

23. अमुद निलैयुं आदित्तन् इयक्कुमुं
कुमुद सकायन् गुणत्तेयुं कूरि

amuda nilaiyum ādittan iyakkamum
kumuda sakāyan guṇatteyum kūri

24. इटैच्चक्करत्तिन् ईरेट्टु निलैयुं
उटर् चक्करत्तिन् उरुपैयुं काट्टि

iṭaiccakkarattin īreṭṭu nilaiyum
uṭarcakkarattin urupaiyum kāṭṭi

20. Rouse the serpent power* which lies latent at the base being the supporting staff of the three mandalas: fire, sun and the moon!

21. Make the sound emanating from the Kundalini* transform into the clear Pranava sound AUM!

22. Teach me the way to rouse the Kundalini* which lies in the fire zone of *Mūlādhāra* through the power of the life breath!

23. Make me understand the blissful state, when the Kundalini reaches *Sahasrāra** as also the paths of *Pingala,* the solar *nadi* and *Ida,* the lunar *nadi.*

24. Make me realise the sixteen states of the Viśuddhi* cakra as also the various facets of *Ashṭānga Yoga*!

---

*To know more about *Kundalini* (Serpent Power), *Muladhara, Sahasrara, Ida, Pingala, Visuddhi cakra* and *Ashtanga Yoga* please refer to my book: *The Holistic Way to Health, Happiness and Harmony,* where these have been dealt with in detail.

राग: खरहरप्रिय Raga: Kharaharapriya

25. षण्मुख तूलमुं चतुर्मुख चूक्कमुं
नण्मुखमाक इनितेनक्कु अरुळिप्

ṣaṇmukha tūlamum caturmukha cūkkamum
naṇmukhamāka initenakku aruḷip

26. पुरियट्ट कायं पुलप्पट एनक्कुत्
तेरियट्टु निलैयुं तेरिशनप्पटुत्तिक्

puriyaṭṭa kāyam pulappaṭa enakkut
teriyaṭṭu nilaiyum teriśanappaṭuttik

27. करुत्तिनिल् कपाल वायिल् काट्टि
इरुत्ति मुत्ति इनितेनक्कु अरुळि

karuttinil kapāla vāyil kāṭṭi
irutti mutti initenakku aruḷi

राग: खमाज Raga: Khamās

28. एन्नै अरिवित्तु एनक्कु अरुळ् चेय्तु
मुन्नै विनैयिन् मुतलै क्कऴ़न्तु

ennai arivittu enakku aruḷ ceytu
munnai vinaiyin mutalaikkazhantu

29. वाक्कुं मनमुं इल्ला मनोलयं
तेक्कियै एन्रन् चिन्तै तेळिवित्तु

vākkum manamum illā manolayam
tekkiye enran cintai teḷivittu

25. Make me understand the significance of the six-letter mantra: *Om Namaśivāya* and the four-letter mantra: *Om śivāya*.

26. Make me understand the secret of the subtle body comprising the five *Tanmātras** and the eight states.

27. Show me how to attain *Sahasrāra* through thought process and realise the state of liberation!

28. Bless me with self-realisation
and remove the root cause for the evils resulting from birth!

29. Grant me the state of *Manolaya* which is beyond speech and thought and make my mind pure and serene!

**Tanmātras* are subtle elements, which are the building blocks of the objective world.

30. इरुळ्वेळि इरण्डुक्कु ओन्रिडं एन्न
अरुळ्तरुं आनन्दत्तु अऴुत्ति एन् चेवियिल्

iruḷveḷi iraṇḍukku onriḍam enna
aruḷ tarum ānandattu azhutti en ceviyil

रागः सुरुटि — Raga: Suruṭi

31. एल्लै इल्ला आनन्दं अळित्तु
अल्लल् कळैन्ते अरुळ् वऴि काट्टिच्

ellai illā ānandam aḷittu
allal kaḷainte aruḷ vazhi kāṭṭic

32. चत्तत्तिन् उळ्ळे सदाशिवं काट्टिच्
चित्तत्तिन् उळ्ळे शिवलिङ्गं काट्टि

cattattin uḷḷe sadāśivam kāṭṭic
cittattin uḷḷe śivalingam kāṭṭi

33. अणुविर्कु अणुवाय् अप्पालुक्कु अप्पालायक्
कणुमुट्ट्रि निन्र करुम्पुळ्ळे काट्टि

aṇuvirku aṇuvāy appālukku appālāyk
kaṇumuṭṭri ninṛa karumpuḷḷe kāṭṭi

रागः मध्यमावति — Raga: Madhyamāvati

34. वेटमुं नीरुं विळङ्कं निरुत्तिक्
कुटुमेय् त्तोण्डर् कुऴात्तुटन् कूट्टि

veṭamum nīrum viḷanka niruttik
kūṭumey ttoṇḍar kuzhāttuṭan kūṭṭi

30. Make me understand the Truth that light and darkness are but facets of the soul
and grant me the bliss (in my ears) resulting from your grace!

31. Show me the path of devotion to bow to your feet and attain endless, limitless, eternal bliss!

32. Show me the awareness of God in sound and the presence of God's form inside the heart!

33. Show the presence of that God who is in the smallest atom as well as the biggest forms of creation, inside me, sweet as sugarcane!

34. Grant me the state of auspiciousness and the way to identify myself with the devotees of the Auspicious Lord and the things which please him like holy ashes etc.

35. अञ्चुक्करत्तिन् अरुं पोरुळ् तन्नै
नेञ्जकूरुत्तिन् निलैयरि वित्तुत्

ancu kkarattin arum poruḷ tannai
nenjakkaruttin nilaiyari vittut

36. तत्तुव निलैयैत्तन्तु एनैयाण्ड
वित्तक विनायक विरैकऴ़ल् शरणे

tattuva nilaiyaittantu enaiyāṇḍa
vittaka vināyaka viraikazhal śaraṇe

35. Make the essence of the Lord whose symbol is the five-letter mantra stand eternal in my mind!

36. O Lord Ganesa, who have no one above you!
You have granted me the true knowledge for God realisation!
I bow to your fragrant feet.
Bless me and grant me your grace!

HYMNS TO GAṆEŚA BY SANKARACHARYA

	Hymn	*Raga*
1.	Gaṇeśa Bhujangam	Ragamalika
2.	Gaṇeśastuti	Ragamalika
3.	Sri Gaṇeśa pancaratnam	Ragamalika

SANKARACHARYA

SANKARACHARYA (788 A.D.–820 A.D.)

Adi Sankara, the Nambudiri Brahmin from Kerala, who lived for only 32 years, was one of the greatest sons of India. He was a philosopher, poet and a mystic saint.

Sankaracharya is more well known as the intellectual philosopher who propounded the philosophy of Advaita, which he did concisely in half a verse: "*Brahma Satyam, Jagat Mithyā, Jīvo Brahmaiva nāparah*" meaning "God, the Supreme, is the only reality, the phenomenal world is an illusion, the individual soul is the same as the Supreme Spirit, not different."

Though Sankara emphasised that knowledge of the identity of the soul with the Supreme was the ultimate means to liberation, he also felt the necessity for devotion to break down the ego and lead to knowledge.

And since devotion necessitated a personal God with attributes (*Saguna Brahman*), he advised people to worship God in six forms (Shanmata), i.e. God visualised as Siva, Sakti, Sun, Vishnu, Kumara or Subrahmanya and as Ganapati.

To facilitate the process of devotion, Sankara composed several beautiful devotional hymns, brimming with poetic ecstasy.

गणेशभुजङ्गम्

रागः हंसध्वनि

Raga: Hamsadhwani

1. रणत्क्षुद्रघण्टानिनादाभिरामं
चलत्ताण्डवोद्दण्डपत्पद्मतालम्।
लसत्तुन्दिलाङ्गोपरिव्यालहारं
गणाधीशमीशानसूनुं तमीडे।।

ranat-kṣudra-ghaṇṭā-ninādābhirāmam
calattāṇḍavoddaṇḍapat-padmatālam
lasattundilāṅgopari vyālahāram
gaṇādhīśamīśānasūnum tam īḍe.

रागः सिंधुभैरवि

Raga: Sindhubhairavi

2. ध्वनिध्वंसवीणालयोल्लासिवक्त्रं
स्फुरच्छुण्ड्दण्डोल्लसद्बीजपूरम्।
गलद्दर्पसौगन्ध्यलोलालिमालं
गणाधीशमीशानसूनुं तमीडे।।

dhvani-dhvamsa-vīṇā layollāsivaktram
sphuracchuṇḍa-daṇḍollasad-bījapūram
galaddarpa-saugandhya-lolālimālam
gaṇādhīśamīśānasūnum tam īḍe.

Gaṇeśa Bhujangam

1. I bow to that Lord of spiritual attendants, son of Siva, who dances, adorned by the garland of jingling bells, keeping rhythm, while dancing, with his lotus-like feet, shining with the moving limbs and the garland of encircling serpent.

2. I bow to that Lord of spiritual attendants, son of Siva, whose face lights up on hearing fine notes of sweet, lute music,
who holds in his trunk the pomegranate fruit,
and who is surrounded by an array of bees eager to taste the fragrance of the rut juice emanating as a result of dancing.

राग: नाट

Raga: Nāṭa

3. प्रकाशञ्जपारक्त रत्नप्रसून
प्रवालप्रभातारुणज्योतिरेकम्।
प्रलम्बोदरं वक्रतुण्डैकदन्तं
गणाधीशमीशानसूनुं तमीडे।।

prakāśaṅ-japārakta-ratna prasūna-
pravāla-prabhātāruṇa-jyotirekam
pralambodaramvakratuṇḍ aika-dantam
gaṇādhīśamīśānasūnum tam īḍe.

राग: मोहनकल्याणि

Raga: Mohanakalyāṇi

4. विचित्रस्फुरद्रत्नमालाकिरीटं
किरीटोल्लसच्चन्द्ररेखाविभूषम्।
विभूषैकभूषं भवध्वंसहेतुं
गणाधीशमीशानसूनुं तमीडे।।

vicitra-sphurad-ratna-mālā-kirīṭam
kirīṭollasac-candra-rekhā-vibhūṣam
vibhūṣaikabhūṣam bhavadhvamsa-hetum
gaṇādhīśmīśānasūnum tam īḍe.

3. I bow to that Lord of spiritual attendants, son of Siva, who is radiant like the red hibiscus flower and the crimson glory of the rising sun, the big bellied One, with the curving trunk and the single tusk.

4. I bow to that Lord of spiritual attendants, son of Siva, who wears a crown, studded with varied, resplendent jewels,
who is adorned with the crescent moon in his crest,
and shines with all the adornment,
and is the cause for the destruction of the phenomenal illusion of birth and death.

रागः कल्याणवसन्तं | Raga: Kalyāṇavasantam

5. उदञ्जद्भुजावल्लरीदृश्यमूलो
च्चलद्भ्रूलताविभ्रमभ्राजदक्षम्।
मरुत्सुन्दरीचामरैः सेव्यमानं
गणाधीशमीशानसूनुं तमीडे।।

udañjad-bhujāvallarī-dṛśyamūlo-
ccalad-bhrūlatā-vibhramabhrāja-dakṣam
marutsundarī–cāmaraiḥ sevyamānam
gaṇādhīśamīśānasūnum tam īḍe.

रागः कुंतालवराळि | Raga: Kuntālavarāḷi

6. स्फुरन्निष्ठुरालोल पिङ्गाक्षितारं
कृपाकोमलोदारलीलावतारम्।
कलाबिन्दुगं गीयते योगिवर्यैः
गणाधीशमीशानसूनुं तमीडे।।

sphuran-niṣṭhurālola-piṅgākṣitāram
kṛpākomalodāra-līlāvatāram
kalābindugam gīyate yogivaryaiḥ
gaṇādhīśamīśānasūnum tam īḍe.

5. I bow to that Lord of spiritual attendants, son of Siva,
whose eyes shine with the knitting of eyebrows due to the lifting up of the trunk
and who is served by the fanning of celestial beauties.

6. I bow to that Lord of spiritual attendants, son of Siva,
who has shining eyeballs within his reddish eyes,
tenderly protects devotees with compassion,
sportingly adopts many manifestations,
and who, located in *Kala* and *Bindu,**
is eulogised by great Yogis and sages.

**Kala* and *Bindu* are centres of creation, according to Hindu thought.

रागः मालहरि | Raga: Mālahari

7. यमेकाक्षरं निर्मलं निर्विकल्पं
गुणातीतमानन्दमाकारशून्यम्।
परं पारमोंकारमाम्नायगर्भं
वदन्ति प्रगल्भं पुराणं तमीडे।।

yam ekākṣaram nirmalam nirvikalpam
guṇātītam ānandam ākāraśūnyam
param pāram omkāram āmnāyagarbham
vadanti pragalbham purāṇam tam īḍe.

रागः मध्यमावति | Raga: Madhyamāvati

8. चिदानन्दसान्द्राय शान्ताय तुभ्यं
नमो विश्वकर्त्रे च हर्त्रे च तुभ्यम्।
नमोऽनन्तलीलाय कैवल्यभासे
नमो विश्वबीज प्रसीदेशसूनो।।

cidānandasāndrāya śāntāya tubhyam
namo viśvakartre ca hartre ca tubhyam
namo'nanta-līlāya kaivalyabhāse
namo viśvabīja prasīdeśasūno.

7. I bow to that primal, primordial Lord,
the unique one, eternal, pure, changeless,
beyond attributes, embodiment of bliss and formless,
the supreme one, symbolised by the pranava sound, AUM,
is the secret of all the vedas and sacred scriptures,
and who is spoken as the primordial one by the sages!

8. O embodiment of consciousness-bliss!
O serene One!
O creator of the universe! who also destroys it!
O Lord with many sporting manifestations!
who shines as the ultimate goal of liberation!
O seed of the universe! O son of Siva!
Prostrations to you! Prostrations to you!
Be propitious!

राग: मध्यमावति Raga: Madhyamāvati

9. इमं सुस्तवं प्रातरुत्थाय भक्त्या
पठेद्यस्तु मर्त्यो लभेत्सर्वकामान्।
गणेशप्रसादेन सिध्यन्ति वाचो
गणेशे विभौ दुर्लभं किं प्रसन्ने।।

imam sustavam prātar utthāya bhaktyā
paṭhed yastu martyo labhet sarvakāmān
gaṇeśa prasādena sidhyanti vāco
gaṇeśe vibhau durlabham kim prasanne.

9. He who gets up in the morning and recites with devotion,
this auspicious hymn, will attain all that is desired,
by the grace of Gaṇeśa will attain knowledge.
When the Lord Gaṇeśa is pleased, what is impossible to get?

गणेशस्तुति

राग: यमन — Raga: Yaman

1. अजं निर्विकल्पं निराकारमेकं
निरानन्दमानन्दं अद्वैदपूर्णं।
परं निर्गुणं निर्विशेषं निरीहं
परब्रह्मस्वरूपं गणेशं भजेम।।

ajam nirvikalpam nirākāramekam
nirānanda mānandam advaitapūrṇam
param nirguṇam nirviśeṣam nirīham
parabrahmasvarūpam gaṇeśam bhajema.

राग: रीतिगौळ — Raga: Rītigowḷa

2. गुणातीतमानं चिदानन्दरूपं
चिदाभासकं सर्वकं ज्ञानगम्यं।
मुनिध्येयमाकाशरूपं परेशं
परब्रह्मरूपं गणेशं भजेम।।

guṇātītamānam cidānandarūpam
cidabhāsakam sarvakam jnānagamyam
munidhyeyamākāśarūpam pareśam
parabrahmarūpam gaṇeśam bhajema.

Gaṇeśastuti

1. Ajam Nirvikalpam

Let us worship Gaṇeśa, the embodiment of the Supreme God!
who is unborn, changeless, formless, unique,
who is bliss personified, and is complete in nonduality,
the supreme one, attributeless, has no special quality,
is devoid of sin.

2. Guṇātītamānam

Let us worship Gaṇeśa, the embodiment of the Supreme God!
who is beyond attributes, is the embodiment of consciousness-bliss,
who shines in the heart, is the doer of everything, and can be attained through knowledge,
who is meditated upon by sages,
whose form is the ether, the supreme Lord!

रागः देश

Raga: Deśa

3. जगद्कारणं कारणज्ञानरूपं
सुरातिं सुगातिं गणेशं गुणेशं
जगद्व्यापिनं विश्ववन्द्यं सुरेशं
परब्रह्मरूपं गणेशं भजेम।।

jagatkāraṇam kāraṇajnānarūpam
surātim sugātim gaṇeśam guṇeśam
jagadvyāpinam viśvavandyam sureśam
parabrahmarūpam gaṇeśam bhajema.

3. Jagat Kāraṇam

Let us worship Ganesa, the embodiment of the Supreme God,
who is the cause of the universe,
the doyen of angels,
who shows the good path,
the Lord of spiritual attendants, the Lord of qualities,
who pervades the universe,
who is venerated by the universe,
the Lord of the celestials!

श्रीगणेशपञ्चरत्नम

रागः रागमालिका — Raga: Rāgamālikā

रागः हंसध्वनि — Raga: Hamsadhwani

1. मुदा करात्तमोदकं सदा विमुक्तिसाधकं
कलाधरावतंसकं विलासिलोकरक्षकम्।
अनायकैकनायकं विनाशितेभदैत्यकं
नताशुभाशुनाशकं नमामि तं विनायकम्।।

mudā karātta modakam sadā vimuktisādhakam
kalaadharaavatamsakam vilāsiloka rakshakam
anaayakaikanaayakam vināśitebhadaityakam
natāśubhāśunaaśakam namaami tam vinaayakam.

रागः मालहरि — Raga: Mālahari

2. नतेतरातिभीकरं नवोदितार्कभास्वरं
नमत्सुरारिनिर्जरं नताधिकापदुद्धरम्।
सुरेश्वरं निधीश्वरं गजेश्वरं गणेश्वरं
महेश्वरं समाश्रये परात्परं निरन्तरम्।।

natetaraatibhīkaram navoditaarka bhaaswaram
namatsuraari nirjaram nataadhikaapaduddharam
sureśwaram nidheeśwaram gajeśwaram
gaṇéswaram
mahéswaram samaaśraye parātparam nirantaram.

Gaṇeśapancaratnam

1. I bow to that Ganesa,
who happily holds a cake in his hand,
is ever the means to liberation,
who is crescent crested and protects persons who sing his praises,
who becomes the leader of leaderless people,
who destroyed the demon elephant,
who quickly eliminates the sins of those who prostrate before him,
the One who has no leader above him (being himself the primordial leader).

2. I ever seek refuge in that Ganesa,
who creates fear in those who do not bow to him,
who is radiant as the newly risen sun,
who wipes out the enemies of angels, who bow before him,
who frees from afflictions those who bow to him,
the Lord of angels, the Lord of hidden treasures,
the Lord of elephants,
the Lord of Ganas,
the great Lord!

रागः कल्याणवसन्तं — Raga: Kalyāṇavasantam

3. समस्तलोकशंकरं निरस्तदैत्यकुञ्जरं
दरेतरोदरं वरं वरेभवक्त्रमक्षरम्।
कृपाकरं क्षमाकरं मुदाकरं यशस्करं
मनस्करं नमस्कृतां नमस्करोमि भास्वरम्।।

samasta loka śankaram nirastadaitya kunjaram
darétarodaram varam varébhavaktramaksharam
kṛpaakaram kshamaakaram mudaākaram yaśaskaram
manaskaram namaskṛtām namaskaromi bhāsvaram.

रागः कुंतालवरालि — Raga: Kuntālavarāli

4. अकिंचनार्तिमार्जनं चिरंतनोक्तिभाजनं
पुरारिपूर्वनन्दनं सुरारिगर्वचर्वणम्।
प्रपञ्चनाशभीषणं धनंजयादिभूषणं
कपोलदानवारणं भजे पुराणवारणम्।।

akincanārtimaarjanam cirantanokti bhaajanam
puraaripūrva nandanam suraari garvacarvaṇam
prapancanaaśa bhīshaṇam dhanamjayaadi bhūshaṇam
kapola daanavaaraṇam bhajé puraaṇavaaraṇam.

3. I bow to that Radiant One,
who does good to all the worlds,
who destroyed the demon elephant,
the big bellied One,
the venerable One,
whose face is like that of *Iravata* (Indra's elephant),
the indestructible One,
who creates compassion, patience, bliss, fame,
and a good heart in those who bow to him.

4. I worship the ancient Elephant-faced One,
who dispels the poverty of his devotees,
the One venerated by the immortal Vedic chants,
the elder son of the enemy of Tripura (Siva),
who put down the arrogance of the enemies of angels,
who frightens the destroyer of the universe (Yama),
who is worshipped by Arjuna and others at the commencement of projects leading to victory,
the destroyer of diseases of the cheeks!

रागः मध्यमावति Raga: Madhyamāvati

5. नितान्तकान्तदन्तकान्तिमन्तकान्तकात्मजं
अचिन्त्यरूपमन्तहीनमन्तरायकृन्तनम्।
हृदन्तरे निरन्तरं वसन्तमेव योगिनां
तमेकदन्तमेव तं विचिन्तयामि सन्ततम्।।

nitaanta kaanta danta kaanti manta kaanta kaatmajam
achintyarūpamanta heenamantaraaya kruntanam
hrudantare nirantaram vasantaméva yoginaam
tamékadantameva tam vichintayaami santatam.

6. महागणेशपञ्चरत्नमादरेण योऽन्वहं
प्रजल्पति प्रभातके हृदि स्मरन् गणेश्वरम्।
अरोगतामदोषतां सुसाहितीं सुपुत्रतां
समाहितायुरष्टभूतिमभ्युपैति सोऽचिरात्।।

mahaa gaṇéśa pancaratna maadaréṇa yo'nvaham
prajalpati prabhaataké hṛdi smaran gaṇeśwaram
arogataamadoshatām susaahiteem suputrataam
samaahitaayurashṭa bhūtimabhyupaiti so'cirāt.

5. I ever think of the unique One,
radiant with beautiful tusk,
the son of the Destroyer of death (Siva),
whose form is unimaginable,
the endless One,
who removes all obstacles,
who ever resides in the hearts of Yogis,
and who has only one tusk.

6. He who recites this prayer of five verses in honour of Ganesa, with veneration daily at dawn, meditating on the Lord of Ganas, attains shortly freedom from ill-health, freedom from sin, proficiency in languages, good children, long life span, and all the eight forms of abundance (wealth, grains, progeny, good fortune, knowledge, victory, valour and fortitude).

HYMN TO GAṆEŚA BY JNANESWAR

	Hymn	*Raga*
1.	Om Namoji Ādya	Lalat

JNANESWAR

JNANESWAR (1275–1296 A.D.)

Jnaneswar was the famous mystic philosopher-poet-saint of Maharashtra, who, despite a short life of 22 years, has bequeathed a legacy of immortal works that remains an inspiration to the people of Maharashtra to this day.

His three important works are: *Jnāneswari*, a monumental yet simple commentary on the Bhagavat Gita, *Anubhavamrita*, in which he explains his philosophy of life and *Abhangs* or devotional lyrics.

Jnaneswar may be considered the philosophic founder of the Bhakti movement in Maharashtra, of which other luminaries are: Namdev (a contemporary of Jnaneswar), Eknath and Tukaram. Jnaneswar's ideal of Bhakti is unique. It is not merely a subjective feeling, but the heart of reality, the *summum bonum* of life. Bhakti or God-devotion or God-intoxication is the root of all moral qualities.

Jnaneswar saw no conflict between Bhakti and the concept of Advaita.

The universe is, according to Jnaneswar, an expression of God's love for Himself.

As water sports with itself in the form of waves, the *ātman* or the Universal Soul plays with itself in the form of the universe and feels happy. God has become man to experience His own affection. One need not forsake the world to find God.

Human life is a precious gift of God. It should be kept pure and holy. The summit of all virtues is God-devotion. There is no object of love greater than God.

In the pathway of loving devotion, the organs of the senses and the tempers of the mind are turned towards God and become vehicles of His love.

According to Jnaneswar, the God-intoxicated become like moons without spots and suns without the scorching heat. Jnaneswar's religion of love is a unique contribution to mankind.

राग: ललात　　　　Raga: Lalāt

1. ॐ नमोजी आद्या। वेदप्रतिपाद्या।।
जय जय स्वसंवेद्या। आत्मरूपा।।१।।
देवा तूचि गणेशू। सकलमति प्रकाशू।।
महाणोनि निवृत्तिदासू। अवधारिजोजी।।२।।
आकार चरण युगुळ। उकार उदर विशाल।।
मकार महामंडल। मस्तकाकारे।।३।।
हे तिन्ही एकवटले। तें शब्दब्रह्म धवळले।।
ते मिमा श्री गुरु कृपा नमिळे। आदिबीज।।४।।

om namojī ādyā. véda pratipādyā.
jaya jaya swasamvédyā. ātmarūpā.
devā tūci gaṇéśū. sakalamati prakāśū.
mahāṇoni nivrittidāsū. avadhārijojī.
ākāra caraṇa yuguḷa. ukāra udara viśāla.
makāra mahāmaṇḍala. mastakākāre.
hé tinhī ékvaṭalé. tém śabdabrahma dhavaḷalé.
té mimā śrī guru kripā namiḷé. ādibīja.

1. Om Namojee aadyaa

   Prostrations to the Primordial Eternal One, discussed by the Vedas! Victory to You! O! Lord who are selfborn and reside in me and all living beings! You are Lord Ganesa! who shine as the beacon of knowledge! Accept my humble prayer and grant beatitude!

   Your feet form the letter A, your large stomach the letter U and your shining crest is the letter M. The combination of the three: AUM, the Pranava Sound is the holy beginning of the universe! With blessings from my Auspicious Guru, I bow before this primordial seed of the universe!

HYMNS TO GAṆEŚA BY ARUNAGIRINATHAR

	Hymn	*Raga*
1.	Umpartarutenumanik	Anandabhairavi
2.	Kaittala Nirai Kani	Nata

ARUNAGIRINATHAR

ARUNAGIRINATHAR (15th Century A.D.)

Biographical details about Arunagirinathar are scanty. He is believed to have been born in Tiruvannamalai, the famous pilgrim centre, in which is located the Siva Temple known for its *Jyotirlinga*.

Arunagirinathar was a profligate in his youth, who suddenly transformed himself into a realised soul and became a devotee of Lord Subramania (or Kumara, as he is known in North India).

Hymns of devotion burst forth from him and he composed over 16000 hymns, of which only 1307 are available today. These hymns are known as *Tiruppugazh*, which means in Tamil Holy Praise of God.

The songs included in this volume are from *Tiruppugazh*. Arunagirinathar has written a few other small works as well, like *Kandaranubhoothi, Kandarandadi, Kandaralankaram* and *Tiruvarutpa*.

Most of his hymns were composed extempore during his visit to the various temples of Lord Subramania in India and Sri Lanka.

Arunagirinathar sang his hymns in Tamil, but he mixed his Tamil expression with a liberal use of Sanskrit and poured forth melodious music, outstanding for its rhythmic patterns.

Arunagirinathar was a saint, a yogi, a poet and a great music composer, apart from being a mystic who felt the presence of his beloved Deity Subramania everywhere. The soul-stirring songs of this saint-singer have electrified subsequent generations and are sung with devotion in musical concerts even today.

राग: आनन्दभैरवि

Raga: Ānandabhairavi

1. उम्पर् तरुतेनुमणिक् कशिवाकि
ओण्कटलिल् तेनमुद त्तुणर्वूरि
इन्पर्सत्ते परुक प्पलकालुं
एन्रनुयिर क्कादरवु ट्ट्ररुळ्वाये
तम्पितनक्काक वन त्तणैवोने
तन्तै वल त्तलारुळ् कैक्कनियोने
अन्पर् तमक्कान निलै प्पोरुळोने
ऐन्तुकरत्तानैमुख प्पेरुमाळे।

umpartarutenumaṇik kaśivāki
oṇkaḍaliltenamudattuṇarvūri
inparsatte paruka ppalakālum
enranuyir kkādaravuṭṭraruḷvāye
tampitanakkāka vanattaṇaivone
tantaivalattālaruḷ kaikkaṇiyone
anpar tamakkāna nilai pporuḷone
eintukarattānaimukha pperumāḷe.

1. Umpartarutenumanik

O Lord with the elephant face, who have five hands! You are more competent in fulfilling the desires of your devotees, than the Kalpa tree, Kamadhenu and the Chintamani stone!
Grant me the grace that true knowledge, which is like the nectar from the milky ocean, should be born in my heart, and growing over the years, give the blissful state of liberation!
For the sake of your brother, you assumed the form of an elephant and went into the forest,*
You walked around your father and got the fruit!**
You are the Supreme One, compassionate towards devotees.

---

*The mythical story is that Ganesa assumed the form of an elephant to frighten Valli, the tribal girl who was the fiancee of his brother, Subramania and force her to seek refuge in the arms of her lover.

**According to legend, there was a contest between the two brothers, Ganesa and Subramania as to who could go round the world faster, the prize being a fruit to be given by the father, Lord Siva. While Subramania set forth to go around the world, Ganesa just went round his parents, who embodied the entire world and thus won the fruit as prize.

Subramania felt cheated and ran away to a hill named Palani and had to be pacified by the parents.

रागः नाट

Raga: Nāṭa

2. कैत्तल निरैकनि अप्पमोडवल्पोरि
कप्पिय करिमुखन् अडिपेणिक्
कट्रिटुं अडियवर् बुद्धियिल् उरैबवर्
कर्पगं येनविनै कडितेगुम्
मत्तमु मदियमुं वैत्तिटुं अरन् मगन्
मरपोरु तिरळ्पुय मदयानै
मत्तळ वयिरनै उत्तमि पुतल्वनै
मट्टविऴ् मलर्कोटु पणिवेने।

kaittala niṛaikani appamoḍaval pori
kappiya karimukhan aḍipéṇik
kaṭriḍum aḍiyavar buddhiyil uṛaibavar
kaṛpagam yenavinai kaḍitégum
mattamumadiyamum vaittiḍum aran magan
maṛporu tiraḷpuya madayānai
mattaḷa vayiṛanai uttami putalvanai
maṭṭavizh malarkoḍu paṇivene.

2. Kaittala niraikani

O! Lord Ganesa! O! Elephant-faced One!
Who appear with your hands full of good eats like fruit, cakes and fried grains,
woes of those who think of you thus will disappear,
their wishes will be fulfilled,
O! Son of Siva, who wear the *datura* flower and
the waxing moon on your head and whose stomach is like the drum
O! Son of Sakti! I worship you with honey dripping flowers!

मुत्तमिऴ् अडैविनै मुऱ्पडु गिरितनिल्
मुर्पड येऴुदिय मुदळ्वोने
मुप्पुरं येरिशेय्द अच्चिवन् उरैरथम्
अच्चतु पोडि शेय्द अतिधीरा
अत्तुयर् अतुकोडु सुब्रमणिपडुं
अप्पुनं अदनिडै इपमागि
अक्कुऱ् मगळुटन् अच्चिरु मुरुगनै
अक्कण मणमरुळ् पेरुमाळे।

muttamizh aḍaivinai muṛpaḍu giritanil
muṛpaḍa yezhudiya mudaḷvoné
muppuram yeriśeyda accivan uṛairatham
accatu poḍi śeyda atidhīrā
attuyar atukoḍu subramaṇipaḍum
appunam adaniḍai ipamāgi
akkuṛamagaḷuḍan acciṛu muruganai
akkaṇa maṇamaruḷ perumāḷé.

O! Lord! You who wrote out the works of Agastya and Vyasa's *Mahabharata*!
O! Courageous One who broke the axle of Lord Siva's chariot,
when He set out to destroy Tripura without first thinking of you!
O! Lord who went to the forest as an elephant and made *Valli* marry *Subramania*!
I worship you with honey dripping flowers.

HYMNS TO GAṆEŚA BY PURANDHARADASA

	Hymn	*Raga*
1.	Saraṇu Siddhi Vinayaka	Yaman
2.	Gajavadana Beduve	Hamsadhwani

PURANDHARADASA

PURANDHARADASA (1484–1564 A.D.)

Purandharadasa, the Kannada saint-musician, was actually a Maratha by birth. He was born in a village near Pune in 1484, the son of a banker.

As a boy, he learnt music and Sanskrit; growing up was married to Saraswatibai, got involved in making money.

Suddenly one day, due to a miracle, the young banker renounced everything and left for Pandharpur and got initiated into asceticism. He travelled to various temples and pilgrim centres all over India and composed devotional songs numbering thousands.

Purandharadasa is considered the Grandfather of Carnatic music. About 8000 of his musical compositions survive today. Purandharadasa's songs extol the mercy of God and are immersed in intense devotion, though replete with references to myths and legends of Sri Krishna.

Having lived a full life of prolific creativity, Purandharadasa died in 1564 at the age of eighty.

Purandharadasa illustrated through his life Tyagaraja's dictum that music and devotion combined make the best path to God-realisation.

राग: यमन | Raga: Yaman

1. शरणु सिद्धिविनायका
शरणु विद्याप्रदायका
शरणु पार्वती प्रणयमूर्ति
शरणु मूषिकवाहना।
निटिल नेत्रने देवी सुतने
नाग भूषण प्रियने
तटिल तांकित कोमलांगने
कर्ण कुण्डल धारने।।

śaraṇu sidhivināyakā
śaraṇu vidyāpradāyakā
śaraṇu pārvatī praṇayamūrti
śaraṇu mūṣikavāhanā
niṭila netrane devī sutane
nāgabhūṣaṇapriyane
taṭilatānkita komalāngane
karṇakuṇḍaladhārane.

1. Śaraṇu siddhivināyaka

You are my refuge, O *Siddhi Vināyaka*, the embodiment of success, who have no leader above you!
You are my refuge, O Granter of learning!
You are my refuge, O Lord who symbolise the love of Parvati!
You are my refuge, O Lord whose vehicle is the mouse!
O Son of Siva (who has the eye on the forehead), and the Divine Mother!
O Lord who love to decorate yourself with snakes!
O Lord who have beautiful limbs!
O Lord who wear rings on your ears!

पट्टमुत्तिन हार पढ़कने
बाहु हस्त चतुष्टने
ईट्ट तोडुगेय हेमकंकण
पाश अंकुश धारने।
कुक्षिमत लंबोदरने
इक्षु चापन गोलिदने
पक्षि वाहन सिरि पुरंधर
विट्टलना निज दासने।।

paṭṭamuttina hāra paḍhakane
bāhu hastacatuṣṭane
īṭṭa toḍugeya hemakankaṇa
pāśa aṃkuśa dhārane
kukṣimatalambodarane
ikṣucāpana golidane
pakṣivāhana siripurandhara
viṭṭalanā nija dāsane.

You wear pearl necklaces
You have four arms!
You wear fine garment and gold bangles!
You hold the noose and the goad!
You have a big belly!
You are fond of food!
You hold the sugarcane bow!
I, the servant of Sri Purandhara Vittal who rides a bird, seek refuge in you.

राग: हंसध्वनि Raga: Hamsadhwani

2. गजवदन बेडुवे
गौरीतनय त्रिजगवन्दितने
सुजनर पोरेवने
पाशाङ्कुशधर परमपवित्र
मूषिक वाहन मुनिजनप्रेमा
मोददिनिन्नय पादवतोरो
साधुवन्दिदने आदरदिन्दलि
सरसिजनाभ श्री पुरन्धरविट्टलन
निरुतनेनयु वन्ते दयमाडो।।

gajavadana beḍuve
gaurītanaya trijagavanditane
sujanaraporevane
pāśāmkuśadhara paramapavitra
mūṣikavāhana munijanapremā
modadininnaya pādavatoro
sādhuvandidane ādaradindali
sarasijanābha śrī purandharaviṭṭalana
nirutanenayu vante dayamāḍo.

2. Gajavadana beduve

O elephant-faced Lord! I beseech you!
O son of Gauri, the fair goddess!
Who are venerated by the three worlds,
O Lord who protect good people!
You hold the noose and the goad! you are extremely pure!
Your vehicle is the mouse!
You are adored by the sages!
Be pleased to show your feet!
Saints worship you with respect!
This servant of Sri Purandhara Vittal,
the Lord with the lotus in his navel, beseeches you!
Show mercy!

HYMN TO GAṆEŚA BY KANAKADASA

	Hymn	*Raga*
1.	Nammamma Sarade	Mohanam

KANAKADASA

KANAKADASA (16th Century A.D.)

Kanakadasa, who was a contemporary of Purandharadasa, was a shepherd by birth. He was a disciple of Vyāsaraya, who was probably Purandharadasa's teacher as well.

Kanakadasa was born in a village named Bada in Dharwar district of Karnataka. His parents died when he was very young and as an orphan was brought up by relatives.

Kanakadasa was devoted to Lord Krishna from childhood. There is a story connected with Kanakadasa and the Udupi temple. Kanakadasa came to the Udupi temple but was denied admission, because of his low caste. He went to the rear of the temple and prayed. As a result of his prayers, the image in the temple turned towards the direction where Kanakadasa was standing and the temple wall collapsed enabling Kanakadasa to have darsan of the Deity. Even today the opening is called *Kanaka's window* at the Udupi Temple.

The Ruler of Anegonde (a part of the Vijayanagar Empire) made Kanaka a chieftain in charge of Bankapur, where he lived and worshipped at the temple of Adi Keshava of Kaginele. Kanakadasa lived for 98 years and travelled throughout the country singing praises of God.

रागः मोहनम् Raga: Mohanam

1. नम्मम्म शारदे उमामहेश्वरि
निम्मोळगिहनारम्मा
कम्म गोलन वैरि सुतनाद सोण्डिल
हेम्मेय गणनाथने।।
मोरे कप्पिन भाव मोरदगलद किवि
कोरे दाडेयनारम्मा।।
मूरु कण्णिन सुत मुरिदिट्ट चन्द्रन
धीरता गणनाथने।।

nammamma śārade umāmahéśwari
nimmoḷagihanārammā
kamma golana vairi sutanāda soṇḍila
hemmeya gaṇanāthané
more kappinabhāva moradagalada kivi
koré dāḍeyanārammā
mūru kaṇṇina suta muridiṭṭa chandrana
dhīratā gaṇanāthané.

1. Nammamma Saarade

O! Mother Sarada! O! Umamaheswari!
Who is this inside you?
He is the son of Siva, the Enemy of Cupid!
He is Ganesa, proud of his trunk!
He has a black-faced form
and has ears like winnow mats!
Mother! Who is this elephant-faced One?
He is the son of the three-eyed Lord Siva,
who broke the pride of the moon!
He is the valiant Ganesa!

उट्टपट्टेय बिगिदुट्ट चल्लणद
दिट्टतानिव नारम्मा। शिवन
पट्टदराणि पार्वतिय कुमारनु
होट्टेय गणनाथने।।
राशि विद्येय बल्ल रमणि हंबल नोल्ल
भाशिगनिव नारम्मा।
लेसागि सुजनर सलहुव कागिनेलियादि
केशवदास काणे।।

uṭṭapaṭṭéya bigiduṭṭa challaṇada
diṭṭatāniva nārammā. sivana
paṭṭadarāṇi pārvatiya kumāranu
hoṭṭeya gaṇanāthane.
rāśi vidyéya balla ramaṇi hambala nolla
bhāśiganiva nārammā.
lesāgi sujanara salahuva kāginéliyādi
kéśavadāsa kāṇé.

Who is this, who wears the loin cloth tight around
his abdomen, Mother?
He is the son of Siva's Queen, Parvati,
the big-bellied Ganesa!
He is the seat of all knowledge, truthful, strong,
courageous and full of compassion!
Who is this eloquent One, Mother?
That He protects good people easily,
this servant of Adi Kesava of Kaginele knows!

HYMN TO GAṆEŚA BY TULSIDAS

	Hymn	*Raga*
1.	Gāyiye Gaṇapati	Yaman

TULSIDAS

TULSIDAS (1532–1623 A.D.)

Details about Tulsidas's life are scanty. He was probably born in 1532 at Rajapur in Uttar Pradesh and lived most of his life—alone and unapproachable—at Varanasi, where he died in 1623. He was a contemporary of Akbar and Rana Pratap Singh of Udaipur.

Tulsidas's most famous work is the *Ramcharitmānas*, which deals with the story of Rama, Prince of Ayodhya, in loving devotion.

Tulsidas was an ardent devotee of Sri Rama as a divine incarnation of God. "The whole universe is full of Mother Sita and Lord Rama. With folded hands, I bow before them", he used to pray.

His other works include: *Krīshna Gītāvali, Vinay Patrikā, Gītāvali, Kavitāvali, Dohāvali* etc. In all these works, Tulsi's devotion to God is explicit.

Tulsidas wrote his poetry in *Lok Bhasha* and *Braj Bhasha,* two dialects of Hindi.

राग: यमन

Raga: Yaman

1. गाइये गणपति जगबंदन
संकर-सुवन भवानी-नंदन।
सिद्धि-सदन, गज-बदन, विनायक।
कृपा-सिंधु, सुंदर, सब लायक।।
मोदक प्रिय, मुद-मंगल दाता।
विद्या बारिधि बुद्धि बिधाता।।
मांगत तुलसिदास कर जोरे।
बसहिं राम सिय मानस मोरे।।

gāyiye gaṇapati jagabandana
sankarasuvana bhavānī nandana
siddhisadana gajabadana vināyaka
kripāsindhu sundar saba lāyaka
modakapriya muda-mangala dātā
vidyā bāridhi buddhi vidhātā
māngata tulasidāsa kara jore
basahi rāma siya mānasa more.

1. Gāyiye gaṇapati jagabandana

Please sing the praises of Ganapati, the Lord of spiritual attendants, who is universally venerated!
Who is the son of Siva, the Creator of bliss, and *Bhavani*, the creatrix,
Who is the abode of accomplishment, Elephant-faced and has no leader above him!
Who is an ocean of mercy!
Who is handsome, and is competent in all things!
Who is fond of rice cakes!
Who is the granter of bliss and auspicious abundance!
Who is the sea of knowledge and guides the intellect!
With folded hands, Tulsidas beseeches such a Ganesa that in the temple of his mind, Lord Rama, accompanied by Sita should ever dwell!*

---

*Even those who worship God in other forms (like Rama in the case of Tulsidas) seek the blessings of Lord Ganesa in getting the grace of their *Istadevata* or favourite Deity.

HYMNS TO GAṆEŚA BY TUKARAM

	Hymn	*Raga*
1.	Omkar pradhan rūp	Yaman
2.	Yei yei ba ganaraya	Patadeep

TUKARAM

TUKARAM (1608–1650 A.D.)

Saint Tukaram was born in a small village named Dehu in Maharashtra in the year 1608. Like his parents, he was a devotee of Vitthal of the temple at Pandharpur.

In his life, Tukaram underwent a lot of misery, including extreme poverty. His family business ran into losses, his first wife died and his second wife, Jijabai, proved to be a shrew. But Tukaram remained unflinching in his devotion to the Lord of Pandharpur and composed mellifluous songs to His Divine Master.

Tukaram's songs are known as *Abhangs* (meaning: unbreakable ones).

What he sang was dutifully recorded by two of his disciples: Gangaram Maval and Santaji Telr and transferred to posterity. Today they are a part of the psyche of the people of Maharashtra.

Tukaram was a contemporary of Shivaji, who was one of his admirers.

Tukaram conducted prayer meetings, singing *bhajans*, to which a large number of people flocked and his fame spread.

He died in 1650.

As one of his disciples declared: No one could match Tukaram in *Jnāna*, *Bhakti* and *Vairāgya* (knowledge, devotion and detachment).

रागः यमन

Raga: Yaman

1. ओंकार प्रधान रूप गणेशाचे
यह प्रिय देवांचे जन्मस्थान
अकार तो ब्रह्म
उकार तो विष्णु
मकार महेश जाणिने ना
ऐसे तेथे देवा जेथो णी उत्पन्ना
तोहाग जो नाथ माय बाप
तुका म्हणे ऐसे आहे वीणावाणी
बहावे पुराणी व्यासाचीया।

omkār pradhān rūp gaṇeśāce
yah priya devānce janmasthān
akār to brahma
ukār to viṣṇu
makār maheś jāṇine nā
eise tethe devā jetho ṇī utpannā
tohāg jo nāth māy bāp
tukā mhaṇe eise āhe vīṇāvāṇī
bahāve purāṇī vyāsācīyā.

1. Omkār pradhān rūp

The pranava sound AUM is the dominant form of Ganesa!
This is the birthplace of the darling deity!
The sound A is Brahmā, the creator,
The sound U is Vishnu, the preserver,
The sound M is Maheśa, the destroyer!
Don't you know this?
The Lord is born of these!
He is my master and my Father!
Tukaram says:
This sweet explanation is according to Vyasa Purana.

राग: पतदीप

Raga: Patadeep

2. येई येई बा गणराया
भेटी देई रे सखाया
नाचत आळे गणपती
घागरया पायी बाजती
अंगी शेंदुराची उटी
केशर तिलक् लल्लाटी
तुका म्हणे पाही पाही
विट्टल गणपती दुजा नाही।

yeī yeī bā gaṇarāyā
bheṭī deī re sakhāyā
nācat āḷe gaṇapatī
ghāgaryā pāyī bājatī
angī śendurācī uṭī
keśar tilak lallāṭī
tukā mhaṇe pāhī pāhī
viṭṭal gaṇapati dujā nāhī.

2. Yei yei bā Gaṇarāya

Please come, please come O Ganesa!
Do come to meet us, O friend!
When Ganapati comes dancing,
the tiny bells of his anklets jingle!
His limbs are covered with vermilion powder!
The saffron mark adorns his forehead!
Tukaram says: Protect me! Protect me!
Lord Vittal and Ganesa are one and the same!

HYMN TO GAṆEŚA BY EKNATH

	Hymn	*Raga*
1.	Omkar Swarupa	Ahirbhairavi

EKNATH

EKNATH (1533–1606 A.D.)

Eknath, the householder saint of Maharashtra was a poet and lover of God, who achieved renunciation, while leading a life of a methodical and self-disciplined householder.

He was probably born in 1533 A.D. in Paithana, Maharashtra.

He lost his parents early and was brought up by his grandparents.

By the age of 12, Eknath had completed reading of Bhagavata. Looking for a spiritual teacher to guide him, he went to Devagad, where a saint named Janardhana Swami took him as a disciple. Eknath worshipped his teacher as God and served him well.

Eknath mentions himself as the disciple of Janardhana in every song of his, in gratitude for his spiritual guidance.

Eknath visited all the sacred shrines and rivers in India, ultimately returning to his hometown Paithana.

As per his Guru's desire, Eknath married Girijabai and lived in Paithana till his death in 1606 A.D., conducting musical discourses and singing the praise of God.

राग: आहिर्भैरवि   Raga: Āhirbhairavi

1. ओंकारस्वरूपा सद्‌गुरु समर्था, अनाथांच्या नाथा, तुज नमो
नमो मायबापा गुरु कृपाघना तोडिया बंधना, माया, मोहा।
मोहजाल माझे कोण नीरशील,
तुजवीण दयाला सदगुरुराया।।
सद्‌गुरुराया माझा आनन्दसागर, त्रैलोक्य आधार गुरुराव।
गुरुराव स्वामी असे स्वयंप्रकाश, ज्यापुढे उदास चंद्र रवी।
रवी शशी अग्नी नेणती ज्या रूपा
स्वप्रकाश रूपा नेणे वेद।।
एका जनार्दनी गुरु परब्रह्मा,
तयाचे पैनाम सदा मुखी।।

omkaara swaroopaa, sadguru samarthaa,
anaathaanchyaa naathaa, tuj namo
namo maayabaapaa gurukripaaghanaa,
toḍiyaa bandhanaa, maayaa, mohaa,
mohajaala maajhe koṇa nīrasheela,
tujaviṇa dayaalaa sadgururaayaa.
sadgururaayaa maajhaa, aanandasaagara,
trailokya aadhaara gururaava,
gururaava swaamī ase swayamprakaasha,
jyaapuḍhe udaasa chandra ravī,
ravī, shashī, agnī, neṇatī jyaa roopā,
swaprakaasha roopaa neṇe veda.
ekaa janaardanī guru parabrahmaa,
tayaache pai naama sadaa mukhī.

1. Omkaar swaroopa

O! Lord whose form is *Aum*, the Pranava sound! O! Great Teacher!
O! Protector of the orphaned! Prostrations to You!
We bow to you, who are our mother, father, teacher and benefactor!
Please break the bonds of illusion and delusion!
Who can clear this entangling web of delusion except You the good, kind guide and teacher? (We bow to you!)
My Lord who are my good teacher! You are the ocean of bliss!
You are the support of the three worlds!
You are self-effulgent!
Before your light, the sun and moon look pale!
The sun, moon and fire do not see this self-effulgent form!
This self-effulgent form is not known even in the Vedas!
Eknath disciple of Janardhana says: The Supreme God is the Teacher and Guide!
His name should always be on our lips!

HYMN TO GAṆ0EŚA BY SAMARTHA RAMADAS

	Hymn	*Raga*
1.	Sukhakarta, dukhaharta	Jogiya

SAMARTHA RAMADAS

SAMARTHA RAMADAS (1608–1681 A.D.)

Samartha Ramadas is one of the five major mystic-saints of Maharashtra, the other four being Jnaneswar, Namdev, Tukaram and Eknath.

Samartha Ramadas was born in 1608 A.D., on the Ramnavami day. His childhood name was Narayan. He ran away from home at the age of eleven, and practised penance on the banks of Krishna river for twelve years. His chosen Deity was Sri Ram. From the age of 24 to 36, he travelled all over India. In the Himalayas, he visited Badrinath, Kedarnath and Kailasanath.

He became a monk and established his Ashram at Chabai on the banks of the Krishna river. His name "Samartha Ramadas" spread far and wide. The Maharashtra Ruler, Shivaji, became his disciple. The story goes that when Ramadas extended his begging bowl, Shivaji put a gift deed of his entire kingdom into it. Ramadas returned it to him, saying: "Rule on my behalf. God bless you!"

Though he himself was a monk, Ramadas did not preach running away from the world to attain spiritual salvation.

According to him one could be active in the material world and yet be spiritual.

राग: जोगिया

Raga: Jogiyā

1. सुखकर्ता दुःखहर्ता वार्ता विघ्नाची।
नुरवी पुरवी प्रेम कृपा जयाची।
सर्वांगी सुंदर ऊटी शेंदुराची।
कंठी झळके माळ मुक्ताफलांची।।
जयदेव जयदेव जय मंगलमूर्ती दर्शन मात्रे मन कामनापूर्ती।।
रत्नखचित फरा तुज गौरीकुमरा।
चंदनाची ऊटी कुंकुमकेशरा।
हिरेजदित मुगुट शोभतो बरा। रुणझुणती नुपुरे चरणी घागरिया
लंबोदर पीतांबर फणिवरबंधना। सरल सोंड वक्रतुंड त्रिनयना।
दास रामाचा वाट पाहे सदना। संकष्टी पावावे निर्वाणी रक्षावे
सुरवरवंदना।।

sukhakartaa, dukhahartaa, vaartaa vighnaachī,
nuravī puravī prema, kripaa jayaachī;
sarvaangī sundara, ootī shenduraachī, kaṇṭhi
jhaḷake maaḷa muktāphalānchī.
jayadeva, jayadeva, jaya mangalamūrtī,
darshanamaatre manakaamanaapoortī.
ratnakhachita pharaa, tuj gaurikumaraa,
chandanaachī ooṭī kumkumakesharaa,
hirejadita muguṭa shobhato baraa, ruṇazhuṇatī
nupure charaṇī ghaagariyaa
lambodara pītaambara phaṇivara bandhanaa,
saralasoṇḍa, vakratuṇḍa, trinayanaa,
daasa raamaachaa vaaṭa paahe sadanaa,
sankashṭi paavaave, nirvaaṇī rakshaave,
suravaravandanaa.

1. Sukhakarta, dukhaharta

O! Lord who create happiness and destroy sorrow, when you hear of obstacles!
Please come, bless us and fill our lives with your love!
You are beautiful in all your limbs, with vermilion smeared on your body and the garland of pearls shining round your neck,
Victory to You! O! Lord! Victory to You! O! Lord with the auspicious form! Please fulfil our desire to see you!
You hold a gem-studded weapon in your hand, O! Son of Mother Gauri!
Your forehead is covered with saffron and vermilion!
The diamond studded crown on your head shines resplendently! the tiny anklet bells on your feet jingle melodiously!
You have a big stomach, and the yellow silken cloth and the snake around your waist.
Your trunk is soft, and curved in shape,
You are three eyed!
Your humble servant Ramadas waits for you at home!
Please protect us in times of trouble and save us in calamity,
O! Lord! venerated by all!
Hail! Hail to You! O! Lord Ganesa with the auspicious form!
Fulfil our desire to have your vision!

HYMNS TO GAṆEŚA BY SHAHJI MAHARAJA

	Hymn	*Raga*
1.	Ceta cintaya	Shubhabandhuvarali
2.	Vande Sivasutam	Padi

SHAHJI MAHARAJA

SHAHJI MAHARAJA (1684 –1710 A.D.)

Shahji Maharaja son of Ekoji Raja the short-lived King of Tanjore—he lived for hardly 26 years—was an intense devotee of the Deity in the temple of Tiruvarur, known as Tyagaraja.

He was a great patron of literature and arts.

He was a masterly scholar in Sanskrit, apart from being proficient in other languages like Telugu, Marathi and Hindusthani.

Shahji's scholarship in Sanskrit and his knowledge of music, combined with his devotion to God, enabled him to compose moving songs set to mellifluous music. All his songs are in Sanskrit.

Shahji Maharaja began the tradition of *nādopāsanā* or practice of music with devotion as a means of God realisation subsequently proved effective by the Trinity of Carnatic music: Tyagaraja, Syama Sastri and Muttuswami Dikshitar.

रागः शुभबन्धुवराळि Raga: Shubhabandhuvarāḷi

1. चेतः चिन्तय सिद्धिबुद्धि समेतम्
धातारमखिलविद्यानां दयाळुं विघ्नराजम्
शरणागतार्ति हरं शशिकलाशेखरम्
करिवरवदनं वरदं भयहरम्
सकलविघ्नतिमिरशमनचण्डकरम्
प्रकटित यशोभरं पर्वतकन्या कुमारम्
विद्या बुद्धि सिद्धये विनुत तनय प्राप्तये
हृद्यश्रेयः प्राप्तये हेरम्ब त्यागकुमारम्।।

cétaḥ ciṅtaya siddibuddhi sametam
dhātāra makhila vidyānām dayāḷum vighnarājam
śaraṇāgatārti haraṁ śaśikalā śekharam
karivara vadanam bhayaharam
sakala vighna timira śamana caṇḍakaram
prakaṭita yaśobharaṁ parvatakaṅyā kumāram
vidyā buddhi siddhaye vinuta tanaya prāptaye
hridyaśreyaḥ prāptaye heraṁba tyāgakumāram.

1. Ceta cintaya siddhibuddhi sametam

O mind! Think of the Lord accompanied by *Siddhi* and *Buddhi* (the deities of achievement and intelligence),
Who is the guardian of all branches of learning, the compassionate Victor over obstacles!
He destroys the afflictions of those who seek refuge, He is crescent crested!
He is elephant faced, granter of boons and destroyer of fears!
His hands can destroy the darkness of all obstacles!
He manifests celebrity, He is the son of the daughter of the mountain, Parvati,
For the sake of acquiring learning and wisdom, and obedient children, and welfare pleasing to the heart, think of the elephant-faced Ganesa, the son who always sacrifices for others.

रागः पाडि

Raga: Pāḍi

2. वन्दे शिवसुतं वरदममरनुतम्।।
सुन्दर गुणयुतं सुप्रसन्नवदनम्।।
बालेन्दुशेखरं फालसिंदूरधरं
लालितभक्तवरं लोलयाविघ्नहरम्
पाशांकुशधरं फणिवरशेखरं
मूषिकवाहनं मोदककरम्।।

vande śivasutam varadamamaranutam
sundara guṇayutam suprasannavadanam
bālenduśekharam phālasindūradharam
lālitabhaktavaram lolayāvighnaharam
pāśāmkuśadharam phaṇivaraśekharam
mūṣikavāhanam modakakaram.

2. Vande sivasutam

I bow to the Son of Siva,
who grants boons and is venerated by the celestials,
I bow to Ganesa,
who is handsome, full of good qualities, and is pleasant faced!
I bow to Lord Ganesa,
who wears the crescent moon on his crest,
and the vermilion mark on his forehead,
who is loved as the darling Deity by great devotees,
and playfully removes obstacles!
who holds the noose and the goad, and wears the serpent chief as ornament,
whose vehicle is the mouse,
and who holds the rice cake in his hands!

HYMNS TO GAṆEŚA BY OOTTUKKADU VENKATA-SUBBA IYER

	Hymn	*Raga*
1.	Ekadanta Vināyakam	Nata
2.	Śrī Vighnarājam bhaje	Hamsadhwani

OOTTUKKADU VENKATASUBBA IYER

OOTTUKKADU VENKATASUBBA IYER (1700–1765 A.D.)

Oottukkadu Venkatasubba Iyer was born in Mannargudi, a village in Tamilnad, around the beginning of the 18th century, the son of Ramachandra Vathoolar and Kamala Nayani Ammal. Though born in Mannargudi, he spent most of his time in the village of Oottukkadu. Hence the name Oottukkadu.

The young Venkatasubban wanted to learn music, but could not find a suitable Guru. His mother asked him to accept Lord Krishna himself as Guru.

He became a mystical devotee of Krishna, kept himself aloof from everyone and composed and sang his songs during the night so as not to be seen or heard by crowds.

He composed over 1000 songs in Tamil and Sanskrit.

When he sang his songs he danced in ecstatic bliss.

Oottukkadu Venkatasubba Iyer was a lifelong celibate and bachelor.

राग: नाट

Raga: Nāṭa

1. एकदन्तविनायकं भजामि मनसा
ईशप्रियकर तनुजं गुरुगुह विनुतं अनिशं
नाग रत्नमणि कुण्डलालङ्कृतं
नव व्याकरण पण्डितादि पूजितं
याग योग जप तप ध्यानादि कार्यवर प्रसिद्धं
सकल लोक पालकं
सङ्गीत शास्त्र रागताळ भावप्रदं सदानन्दसहितं

ekadantavināyakam bhajāmi manasā
īśapriyakaratanujam guruguha vinutam aniśam
nāgaratnamaṇi kuṇḍalālankṛtam
nava vyākaraṇa paṇḍitādi pūjitam
yāgayoga japatapa dhyānādi kāryavara prasiddham
sakalaloka pālakam
samgītaśāstra rāga tāḷa bhāvapradam sadānandasahitam

1. Ekadanta Vināyakam

I worship through my mind
the Lord with one tusk, who has no leader above him,
the son who pleases Siva,
who is ever venerated by Subrahmania,
who is adorned by the serpent, diamonds and other jewels,
who is worshipped by scholars expert in grammar,
who is famous for giving the results of sacrificial rites, and practices like Yoga, chanting of names, penance etc., the Protector of all the worlds,
who gives feeling to musical science, melodies, rhythms etc. and who is ever blissful,

मातङ्गमुखचन्द्रबिम्बवदनं
महात्रिपुर सुन्दरी नन्दनं
आतङ्ग मुख भक्तमनोरथ
अभीष्ट वरप्रदायकं सुन्दरं
नादलोलं निरामय कोशं नळिन विलोचन
रवि कोटि प्रकाशं
वेद निगम सकलागम सन्नुत वितरण
गुणशीलं बालं
वेद वेदान्त बोधकचतुरं व्यासविनुतमहनीयं
वारं वारं वारं
एकदन्तं विनायकं भजामि।

mātangamukha candrabimbavadanam
mahātripurasundarī nandanam
ātangamukha bhakta manoratha
abhīṣṭavarapradāyakam sundaram
nādalolam nirāmayakośam naḷina vilocana
ravikoṭiprakāśam
vedanigama sakalāgama sannuta vitaraṇa
guṇasīlam bālam
vedavedānta bodhakacaturam
vyāsavinutamahanīyam
vāram vāram vāram
ekadantam vināyakam bhajāmi.

the elephant-faced One,
whose face is like the moon,
the son of *Tripura Sundari*, the Divine Mother,
the granter of boons desired by devotees,
whose faces reflect their anguish,
the handsome Lord,
who is interested in sound, the treasure of innocence,
who has tender eyes, and whose radiance equals that of a million suns,
who is venerated in all the sacred scriptures, the Lord full of good qualities, the young lad,
who is competent in teaching all the Vedas and Upanishads,
who is worshipped by Veda Vyasa, the great Lord,
again and again and again, I worship.

राग: हंसध्वनि Raga: Hamsadhwani

2. श्री विघ्नराजं भजे संततमहं कुञ्जरमुखं
शंकर सुतं शंकरीसुतं
संततमहं दन्तिसुन्दरमुखं अन्तकान्तकसुतं
शिवशंकरिसुतं
सेवित सुरेन्द्रमहनीय गुणशीलं
जपतप समाधि सुख वरदानुकूलं
भावित सुरमुनिगण भक्त परिपालं
भयंकर विषंग मातंग कुलकालं

śrī vighnarājam bhaje santatamaham kunjara-mukham
śamkarasutam śamkarīsutam
santatamaham dantisundaramukham antakān-takasutam
śivaśankarisutam
sevita surendramahanīyaguṇaśīlam
japatapasamādhisukhavaradānukūlam
bhāvita suramunigaṇa bhakta paripālam
bhayamkara viṣanga mātanga kulakālam

2. Śrī vighnarājam bhaje

I ever meditate on the auspicious Lord of obstacles who is elephant-faced!
the son of Siva and Sakti, the Creators of bliss, here and now,
Always, I meditate on the Lord with the beautiful elephant face, the son of the Destroyer of the demon *Anthaka*,
the son of Siva and Sakti, the Creators of bliss!
Who is worshipped by the Chief of angels,
who has great qualities,
who is favourably inclined to grant the fruits of various spiritual practices like chants, penance and *Samadhi*,
who protects celestials, sages and devotees who think of him,
the destroyer of the lineage of fearful poisonous elephants,

कनक केयूर हारावलीखलित
गंभीर कौलगिरि शोभं सुशोभं
कामादि भय भरित मूढ़मत
कलिकलुष खण्डितं अखण्ड प्रतापं
सनक शुक नारद पतंजलि पराशर मातंग मुनिसंग सल्लापं
सत्य वर मध्यनयनं प्रमुख मुक्तिकरं
तत्वमसि नित्य निगमादि स्वरूपं
तमिह श्री विघ्नराजं भजेऽहम्।।

kanakakeyūra hārāvalīkhalita
gambhīrakaulagiriśobham suśobham
kāmādi bhaya bharita mūḍhamata
kalikaluṣakhaṇḍitam akhaṇḍa pratāpaṃ
sanaka śuka nārada patanjali parāśara mātanga
muni sangasallāpam
satyavaramadhyanayanam pramukha muktikaram
tatvamasi niṭya nigamādisvarūpam
tamiha śrī vighnarājam bhaje'ham.

who shines in the mountain, with rows of gold armlets and necklaces,
who destroys the dark stains of the Kali age, born of ignorance filled with lust, fear etc.,
who delights chatting in the company of sages like Sanaka, Suka, Narada, Patanjali, Parasara, Matanga etc.,
Chief among the truthful, who has an eye in the middle of the forehead, who gives liberation to the evolved,
whose form embodies the scriptural teaching of Tatvamasi (Thou art That).
I meditate on the Lord of obstacles here and now.

HYMNS TO GAṆEŚA BY TYAGARAJA

	Hymn	*Raga*
1.	Sri Ganapatini Sevimpare	Saurashtra
2.	Girirajasutatanaya	Bangala

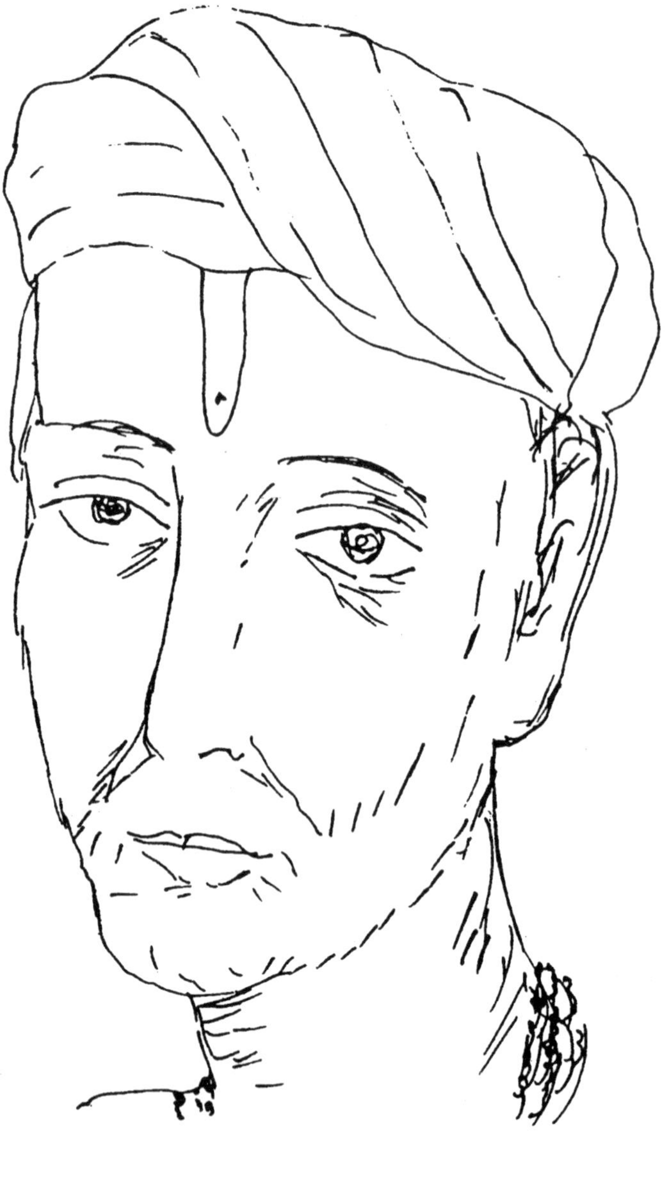

TYAGARAJA

TYAGARAJA (1767–1847 A.D.)

Tyagaraja, the saint composer was born in Tiruvaiyar in Tamil Nadu on 4th May 1767. He lived most of his life in Tiruvaiyar till his death on 6th January 1847.

Right from childhood he devoted himself to the worship of Lord Rama singing songs extolling his favourite deity.

He had a daughter, through whom he had a grandson, who died progeniless. Thus we do not have any descendants of saint Tyagaraja. His wife predeceased him.

Daily Tyagaraja would walk the streets of his native town singing songs and seeking alms (known as *Unchavritti*).

Tyagaraja has composed about 800 songs, most of them in his mother tongue Telugu and a few in Sanskrit.

The only travel he undertook in his life was a short pilgrimage from Tirupati to Srirangam.

Tyagaraja shied away from material possessions and refused to sing in praise of the King. He was determined to remain poor and independent.

Tyagaraja lived his own philosophy that God realisation was best achieved through *Nādopāsanā* (music with devotion). His songs are surfeit with an intimate devotion for Rama, though they fully reveal his deep understanding of the tenets of the Vedas and Upanishads.

राग: सौराष्ट्र Raga: Saurāshṭra

1. श्री गणपतिनि सेविंपरे, श्रितमानवुलारा!
वागाधिपादि सुपूजल चेकनि
बाग नटिंपुचु वेडलिन
पनस - नारिकेलादि - जम्बू - फलमुलारगिंचि
घनतरम्बुगनु महिपै पदमुलु
घल्लुघल्लन नुंचि
अनयमु हरिचरणयुगमुलनु हृदयांबुजमुन नुंचि
विनयमुननु त्यागराज विनुतुडु
त्रिविधगतुल धळंगुमचि वेडालन।

śrīgaṇapatini sevimpare śritamānavulārā!
vāgādhipādi supūjala cekani
bāga naṭimpucu veḍalina
panasa-nārikelādi-jambu-phalamulāramgici
ghanatarambuganu mahipai padamulu
ghallughallana numci
anayamu haricaraṇayugamulanu hṛdayāmbujamuna numci
vinayamunanu tyāgarāja vinutuḍu
trividhagatula dhaḷamgumaci veḍālana.

1. Śrī Gaṇapatini sevimpare

Worship the auspicious Ganapati, Lord of spiritual attendants, noble men of devotion!

Having accepted the worship of Brahma and others,

He is coming, dancing well!

After tasting the offerings of jackfruit, coconut, jambu fruit, He is coming pounding the earth with his heavy resounding steps!

Installing the holy feet of Vishnu in the lotus of his heart,

He is coming dancing in varied rhythms!

Tyagaraja bows to Him in all humility.

राग: बङ्गाळ — Raga: Bangāḷa

2. गिरिराजसुतातनय! सदय!
सुरनाथमुखार्चितपादयुग!
परिपालय! मामिभराजमुख!
गणनाथ! परात्पर! शंकरा-
गमवारिनिधिरजनीकर!
फणिराजकंकण! विघ्ननिवारण!
शाम्भव! श्रीत्यागराजनुत!

girirājasutātanaya! sadaya!
suranāthamukhārcitapādayuga
paripālaya māmibharājamukha
gaṇanātha! parātpara! śamkarā-
gamavārinidhirajanīkara!
phaṇirājakamkaṇa! vighnanivāraṇa!
śāmbhava! śrītyāgarājanuta!

2. Girirājasutā tanaya

O Son of the Goddess, daughter of the mountain king!
O Compassionate One!
Whose pair of feet are worshipped by the Chief of celestials and others!
Protect me, O elephant-faced Lord!
O Lord of spiritual attendants!
O Supreme Lord!
O creator of bliss!
Who are like the moon to the ocean of sacred scriptures!
Who wear the serpent king as a bangle!
O Remover of obstacles!
O Son of Siva, the creator of bliss!
O Lord to whom bows Tyagaraja!

HYMNS TO GAṆEŚA BY MUTTUSWAMI DIKSHITAR

	Hymn	*Raga*
1.	Sri gananatham	Isamanohari
2.	Ganarajen Rakshitoham	Arabhi
3.	Ekadantam bhajeham	Bilahari
4.	Siddhivinayakam	Sama
5.	Mahāganapatim	Todi
6.	Sri Muladharacakravinayaka	Sri
7.	Herambaya namaste	Atana
8.	Vātāpi Ganapatim	Hamsadhwani
9.	Vallabhanayakasya	Begada

MUTTUSWAMI DIKSHITAR

MUTTUSWAMI DIKSHITAR (1775–1835 A.D.)

Like Tyagaraja and Syama Sastri, Muttuswami Dikshitar, one of the Trinity of Carnatic Music, was born in Tiruvarur in the Thanjavur district of Tamil Nadu.

Inheriting music knowledge from his father, Muttuswami Dikshitar embellished it with his mastery of the Sanskrit language.

One special feature about the songs of Dikshitar is that they are all related to and centre around Deities in various temples in South India, to which he made pilgrimages throughout his life of sixty years.

Muttuswami Dikshitar composed his first song at the Subrahmanya temple at Tiruttani. He considered the Deity of this temple as his Guru and hence used the pen-name "Guru Guha" in all his musical compositions.

The major temples visited by Dikshitar and on whose deities he composed songs are: Tirupati, Kalahasti, Kancheepuram, Chidambaram, Madurai, Sri Rangam, Kumbhakonam, Tirunelveli, Rameswaram, Tiruchendur, Sabarimalai apart from Tiruvarur, his own hometown.

Though Bhakti or devotion is the main ingredient in his songs, this is tempered by *Jnana* or knowledge.

Muttuswami Dikshitar was a Vedantin, in the tradition of Sankara, who believed in One Supreme Power and considered the deities worshipped as manifestations of that Supreme Power, who transcended name and form.

The songs of Dikshitar, composed in chaste Sanskrit and set to a variety of majestic tunes (both Carnatic and Hindustani), exude a feeling of serenity, dignity and bliss,

राग: ईशमनोहरि — Raga: Īśamanohari

1. श्री गणनाथं भज रे चित्त पराशक्तिसुतम्
नागयज्ञसूत्रधरं नादलयानन्दकरम्
आगमादिसन्नुतं अखिल लोक पूजितं
योगीशादि भावितं भोगीशायिसेवितं
राग द्वेषादि रहित रमणीय हृदयमुदितं
श्री गुरुगुह सम्मुदितं चिन्मूल कमलाश्रितम्।

śrī gaṇanātham bhaja re citta parāśaktisutam
nāgayajnasūtradharam nādalayānandakaram
āgamādisannutam akhilalokapūjitam
yogīśādibhāvitam bhogīśāyisevitam
rāgadveṣādirahitaramaṇīyahṛdayamuditam
śrī guruguha sammuditam cinmūlakamalāśritam.

characteristic of a truly evolved spiritual savant.

1. Śrī Gaṇanātham

O mind! Meditate on the auspicious Lord of spiritual attendants, the son of the Supreme Power, the Divine Mother,
who wears the serpent as the sacred thread,
who rejoices in the merger of melodies,
who is venerated in the sacred scriptures,
who is worshipped by the whole world,
who is thought of by chiefs of Yogis,
who is served by Visnu, who lies on the serpent-chief,
who is happy with beautiful hearts,
who is devoid of evils like passion, hatred etc.,
who is rendered happy by Subrahmania,
who is located in the lotus of Muladhara.*

---

*The belief in India is that God dwells in the hearts of all beings (*Hrdayakamalavāsī*) (akin to Christ's assertion that "the kingdom of God is within you").

In this inner kingdom of consciousness, there are six psychic centres: Mūlādhāra, Svādhistāna, Manipura, Anahata, Visuddhi and Ajna. Various forms of God are associated with the different cakras or psychic centres.

Thus Ganesa is deemed to reside in Muladhara, Brahmā in Svādhistana, Viṣṇu in Manipura, Rudra in Anahata and so on.

राग: आरभि

Raga: Ārabhi

2. गण राजेन रक्षितोहम् गुणिजन नुत पल्लव पदेन
अणिमाद्यष्ट सिद्धिप्रदेन माणिक्यमकुटादिधरेण
मन्त्रिणी पूजित सुमुखेन मानित गुरु गुह वन्दितेन
दिनकर कोटि प्रकाशेन विनताश्रित मन्दारेण
मनु पूजित पाशाङ्कुशेन कानन स्थित ब्रह्मचर्येण
गणराजेन रक्षितोहम्।

gaṇarājena rakṣitoham guṇijananutapallavapadena
aṇimādyaṣṭasiddhipradena māṇikyamakuṭādidhareṇa
mantriṇīpūjita sumukhena mānitaguruguha vanditena
dinakarakoṭi prakāśena vinatāśrita mandāreṇa
manupūjita pāśāṁkuśena kānanasthita brahmacaryeṇa
gaṇarājena rakṣitoham.

2. Gaṇsarājena Rakṣitoham

I am protected by the Ruler of spiritual attendants,
whose tender feet are worshipped by good people,
who gives the eight occult powers like Anima etc.,
who wears bejewelled crown,
whose pleasant face is worshipped by those who know sacred prayers,
to whom bows the venerated Subrahmania,
whose radiance equals that of a million suns,
in whom the humbled elephants sought refuge,
whose noose and goad were worshipped by *Manu*,
the celibate who stays in the forests,
I am protected by the Ruler of spiritual attendants.

रागः बिलहरि | Raga: Bilahari

3. एकदन्तं भजेऽहं एकानेक फलप्रदं
पाकसरसनाराधितं पामर पण्डितादि नुतपदं
कैलासनाथ कुमारं कार्तिकेय मनोहरं
हालास्य क्षेत्र वेगवती तटविहारं हरं
कोलाहल गुरुगुह सहितं कोटि मार लावण्यहितं
माला कङ्कणादि धरणं माया वल्लभाम्बा रमणं।

ekadantam bhaje aham ekānekaphalapradam
pākasarasanārādhitam pāmarapaṇḍitādinutapadam
kailāsanāthakumaram kārtikeyamanoharam
hālāsyakṣetra vegavatitaṭavihāram haram
kolāhalaguruguhasahitam koṭimāralāvaṇyahitam
mālākankaṇādidharaṇam māyāvallabhāmbāramaṇam.

3. Ekadantam bhajeham

I worship the Lord with the single tusk,
who grants myriad boons,
who is worshipped by Indra,
at whose feet prostrates everyone from the common man to the learned pundits,
who is the son of Siva, the Lord of Kailasa,
who won the heart of *Kartikeya*,
who resides on the bank of the river *Vegavati* in the region of *Hālāsya*,
the destroyer (of sin, sorrow and obstacles),
who is joyfully accompanied by Subrahmania,
who is attractive like a million gods of love,
who wears garlands and bangles,
who sports with Mother *Vallabhā*, who is Māyā.*

This is a song sung about the Ganesa image in the temple of Madurai.

*Though Lord Ganesa is a confirmed bachelor, many myths and legends attribute several symbolic spouses for him. Thus Siddhi and Buddhi, success and intellect, are considered symbolic spouses of Ganesa.

Vallabha is a synonym for *Māyā*, the elusive feminine power which transforms the formless Infinite into diversified creation. Ganesa being identified with the Supreme Godhead and as the source of creation is deemed to be the spouse of Vallabha or Maya.

रागः शाम Raga: Śāma

4. सिद्धिविनायकं अनिशं चिन्तयाम्यहं
प्रसिद्ध गणनायकं विशिष्टार्थ दायकं वरं
सिद्ध यक्ष किन्नरादि सेवितं अखिल जगत्-
प्रसिद्धं मूलपङ्कज मध्यस्थं मोदक हस्तं
भाद्रपद मास चतुर्थ्यां ब्राह्मणादि पूजितं।

siddhivināyakam aniśam cintayāmyaham
prasiddha gaṇanāyakam viśiṣṭārthadāyakam varam
siddhayakṣakinnarādisevitam akhilajagat-
prasiddham mūlapaṃkajamadhyastham modakahastam
bhādrapadamāsacaturthyām brāhmaṇādipūjitam.

4. Siddhivināyakam

I ever think of Siddhi Vinayaka, the Lord who has no leader above him and who is the embodiment of success,
who is the reputed master of spiritual attendants,
the noble one who grants special boons,
who is worshipped by *siddhas, yakshas* and *kinnaras,*
who is famous in all the worlds,
who is seated in the lotus of *Muladhara,*
who has the rice cake in his hand,
who is worshipped by Brahmins on the fourth day (after full moon) in the month of *Bhadrapada.*

रागः तोडि Raga: Toḍi

5. महा गणपतिं वन्दे माधवाद्यमरबृन्दम्
अहन्तादिरहितं शक्तिविहितं आनन्ददन्तमेकदन्तं
त्रिपुरवधार्थं शिवेन त्र्यम्बकेनार्चितं उपनिषत्प्रतिपादितं
उमामहेश्वरसुतं
कपिल वसिष्टादिनतं कंजजातिभिरीडितं कपिलं
कृष्ण पूजितं करिवदनेन शोभितं
सुपर्णवाह सेवितं सुरगुरुगुह भावितं कपिताम्रपनस
जम्बूकदलीफलभक्षितं
महागणपतिं वन्दे

mahāgaṇapatim vande mādhavādyamaravṛndam
ahantādirahitam śaktivihitam
ānandadantamekadantam
tripuravadhārtham śivena tryambakenārcitam
upaniṣadpratipāditam umāmaheśvarasutam
kapilavasiṣṭādinatam kamjajātibhirīḍitam kapilam
kṛṣṇapūjitam karivadanena śobhitam
suparṇavāhasevitam suraguruguhabhāvitam
kapitāmrapanasa
jambūkadalīphalabhakṣitam
mahāgaṇapatim vande

5. Mahāgaṇapatim

I bow to that great Lord of spiritual attendants,
who is surrounded by Vishnu, the Lord of Lakshmi and other angels,
who is devoid of evils like the ego,
who was formed by Sakti, the Divine Mother, the Granter of bliss, the Lord with a single tusk,
who was worshipped by the three-eyed Siva in order to destroy the demons Tripura,
The one who has been mentioned in the Upanishads,
the son of Uma and Maheswara, the great Lord,
who is venerated by sages like *Kapila* and *Vasishta*,
who is eulogised by *Brahma* and others,
who is copper-hued,
the one worshipped by *Krishna*, and shines with the elephant face,
the one worshipped by *Vishnu*, whose vehicle is Garuda, the bird
who is meditated upon by celestials and Subrahmania,
who eats fruits like the rose apple, mango, jackfruit, banana etc.

पाशाङ्कुश धरं छत्रचामर परि वीजितं
रौद्र भाव रहितं दासजनहृदय विराजितं
रौहिणेयानुजार्चितं ईहना वर्जितं
अद्रिराजसुतात्मजं अनन्तगुरुगुहाग्रजं
भद्रप्रद पदाम्बुजं भासमान चतुर्भुजं।

pāśāmkuśadharam chatracāmaraparivījitam
raudrabhāvarahitam dāsajanahṛdayavirājitam
rauhiṇeyānujārcitam īhanāvarjitam
adrirājasutātmajam anantaguruguhāgrajam
bhadraprada padāmbujam bhāsamānacaturbhujam.

who holds the noose and the goad,
who is served with the fan and the umbrella,
who is devoid of anger,
who shines in the hearts of devotees,
who is worshipped by *Krishna,* the younger brother of *Balarāma* the son of *Rohini,*
who is devoid of greed,
the son of *Pārvati,* daughter of the mountain king,
the elder brother of the immortal Subrahmania,
whose feet bestow auspicious prosperity,
the four-armed One!

राग: श्री

Raga: Śrī

6. श्री मूलाधार चक्रविनायक अमूल्यवरप्रदायक
मूलाज्ञानशोक विनाशक मूल कन्द मुक्तिप्रदायक
सकळीकृत देवादि देव शबळी कृत सर्वज्ञ स्वभाव
प्रकटीकृत वैखरी स्वभाव पराभव प्रसिद्धगजग्रीव
विकट षट्शतंश वासाधिकार विचित्राकार भक्तोपकार
अकलङ्क विभा स्वर विघ्नेश्वर हरगुरुगुहसोदर लम्बोदर।

śrīmūlādhāracakravināyaka amūlyavarapradāyaka
mulājnānaśokavināśaka mūlakandamuktipradāyaka
sakaḷīkṛtadevādideva sabaḷīkṛtasárvajnasvabhāva
prakaṭīkṛta vaikharī svabhāva parābhava prasiddha-gajagrīva
vikaṭaṣaṭśatamśa vāsādhikāra vicitrākārabhaktopakāra
akalankavibhāsvara vighneśvara haraguruguhasodara lambodara.

6. Śrī mūlādhāracakra Vināyaka

O lord who have no leader above you,
who are located in the Muladhara cakra,
You grant invaluable boons!
You destroy the sorrows arising out of the roots of ignorance!
You are the primal cause of everything!
You grant liberation!
You are the Lord above all angels,
who is the master of varied knowledge!
who makes clear the form of speech known as *Vaikhari*,
O peerless One!
You are the famous elephant-faced One!
You are huge!
You rule over six hundred breaths,
Your form is peculiar!
You aid your devotees always!
You shine with stainless radiance!
You are the Lord of obstacles!
You are the brother of Subrahmania, who was the teacher to Siva,
You have a big belly!
O Lord located in the Muladhara cakra!

राग: अटाना

Raga: Aṭānā

7. हेरम्बाय नमस्ते हरिब्रह्मेन्द्रादि सेविताय शिवकुमाराय
वीर गणादिमुदिताय वीरादि वरप्रदाय
सूरिजनोपासिताय सुरगुरुगुह सेविताय
परमेश्वरकुमाराय पञ्चहस्ताय पाशाङ्कुशधराय
प्रसिद्ध गण नाथाय विनायकाय नमस्ते।

herambāya namaste haribrahmendrādisevitāya śivakumārāya
vīragaṇādimuditāya vīrādivarapradāya
sūrijanopāsitāya suraguruguhasevitāya
parameśvarakumārāya pancahastāya pāsāmkuśadharāya
prasiddhagaṇanāthāya vināyakāya namaste.

7. Herambāya namaste

Prostrations to the heroic One!
who is worshipped by Visnu, Brahma and others!
the Son of Siva,
who renders happy the heroic spiritual attendants of Siva,
who grants boons like valour!
who is meditated upon by the celestials,
who is worshipped by the lordly Subrahmania!
the son of the Supreme Lord, Siva,
the five-armed One!
who holds the noose and the goad!
the reputed Lord of spiritual attendants!
the Lord who has no leader above him!
Prostrations to the heroic One!

राग: हंसध्वनि

Raga: Hamsadhwani

8. वातापि गणपतिं भजेऽहं वारणास्यं वरप्रदं श्री
भूतादि संसेवित शरणं भूत भौतिक प्रपञ्च भरणम्
वीतरागिणं विनतयोगिनं विश्वकारणं विघ्नवारणम्
पुराकुंभसंभव मुनिवरप्रपूजितं त्रिकोण मध्यगतम्
मुरारि प्रमुखाद्युपासितं मूलाधार क्षेत्रस्थितम्
परादिचत्वारिवागात्मकं प्रणवस्वरूपवक्रतुण्डम्
निरन्तरं निटिल चन्द्रखण्डं निजवामकर विधृतेक्षुदण्डम्
करांबुज पाश बीजापूरं कलुषविदूरं भूताकायम्
हरादि गुरुगुह तोषित बिंबं हंसध्वनिभूषित हेरंबम्।

vātāpi gaṇapatim bhajéham vāraṇāsyam varapradam śrī
bhūtadi samsévita śaraṇam bhūta bhautika prapanca bharaṇam
vītarāgiṇam vinatayoginam viśvakāraṇam vighnavāraṇam
purā kumbha sambhava munivaraprapūjitam trikoṅa madhyagatam
murāri pramukhādyupāsitam mūlādhāra kṣétra sthitam
parādicatwārivāgātmakam praṇava swarūpa vakra tuṇḍam
nirantaram niṭila candrakhaṇḍam nijavāmakara vidhritekṣudaṇḍam
karāmbuja pāśa bījāpūram kaluṣavidūram bhūtākāyam
harādi guruguha toṣita bimbam hamsadhwani bhūṣita hérambam.

8. Vātāpi Gaṇapatim

I worship Vātāpi Gaṇapati,* who is elephant faced, grants boons and is ever auspicious!
I worship Him, whose feet are worshipped by the Elemental Powers, who bears the five elements of earth, water, air, fire and ether and the worlds created out of them,
who is without passion, to whom the Yogis bow down, the cause of the universe, the Remover of obstacles.
I worship Vatapi Ganapati, who was in ancient past worshipped by the great sage Agastya, who is seated in the centre of the triangular yantra,
who is meditated upon by Vishnu and other prominent persons, who is situated in the Mooladhara cakra,
who exists in the four modes of speech: *Para, Pasyanti, Madhyama* and *Vaikhari*,
whose form is the Pranava sound: AUM,
who has a curving trunk,
who always has the crescent moon on the forehead,
who holds the sugarcane stump in His left hand,
who has in His lotus hands: the rope, pomegranate fruit, guava etc.,
the sinless One,
who has a gigantic form,
whose form pleases Siva, Subrahmanya and others,
who is pleased by the raga *Hamsadhwani*,
the Elephant-faced One!

* Vātāpi Ganapati is the Deity in Tiruvarur, the hometown of Dikshitar.

रागः बेगड Raga: Begaḍa

9. बल्लभानायकस्य भक्तो भवामि वाञ्छितार्थ दायकस्य
वरमूषिक वाहनस्य
पल्लवपद मृदुतरस्य पाशाङ्कुशादि धरस्य
मल्लिका जाती चंपक हारस्य मणिमालस्य
वल्ली विवाह कारणस्य गुरुगुह पूजितस्य
काळीकला मालिनी कमलाक्षि सन्नुतस्य।

vallabhaa nāyakasya bhakto bhavaami vānchitārtha dāyakasya
vara mūṣika vāhanasya
pallava pada mṛdu tarasya pāśānkuśādi dharasya
mallikā jātī campaka hārasya maṇimālasya
vallī vivāha kāraṇasya guruguha pūjitasya
kāḷīkalāmālinī kamalākṣi sannutasya.

9. Vallabha Nayakasya

I am the devotee of the Lord of Vallabhaa, who gives whatever is desired!
And whose vehicle is the great mouse!
I am the devotee of the One whose feet are soft like tender shoots!
Who holds the rope and the axe!
Who wears the garland of jasmine and champak flowers as also of gems!
Who was the cause of *Valli*'s marriage!
Who is worshipped by Subrahmanya!
Who is venerated by Kaali, Sarasvati and the lotus-eyed Lakshmi!

HYMNS TO GAṆEŚA BY RAMALINGA SWAMIGAL

	Hymn	*Raga*
1.	Munnavane	Nata
2.	Nadamumkatantu	Hamsadhwani
3.	Kanalneervizhainta	Sindhubhairavi
4.	Munnaruntavatton	Sri
5.	Tiruvum kalviyun	Hindolam
6.	Seetanaanmalar	Ritigowla
7.	Tanjamenrunai	Deś
8.	Kallanencakan	Suddhasaveri
9.	Mannilasai	Yamunakalyani
10.	Aanileyanri	Suruti
11.	Navinalunai	Madhyamavati

RAMALINGA SWAMIGAL

RAMALINGA SWAMIGAL (1823–1874 A.D.)

Ramalinga Swamigal was a Saivite mystic who preached the universal religion of humanity: *Samarasa Suddha Satya Sanmārga*.

Ramalinga Swami, though of the nineteenth century A.D., was in the line of the Tamil Mystics of an earlier age like *Tirumūlar, Mānikkavachakar, Sambandhar, Appar, Sundarar, Pattinattār, Arunagirināthar* and *Tāyumanavar*.

He was a God-intoxicated, God-realised saint who poured out lyrics soaked in intense devotion.

His most famous work *Tiru Arutpa* can stand comparison with classics like *Tiruvāchakam* and *Tirumantiram*.

The songs of Ramalinga Swamigal will be included in a subsequent volume of the Sacred Songs of India. But his hymns to Ganesa included in this volume will give a sampling of his intense spiritual fervour.

In the words of Professor K.R. Srinivasa Iyengar, "radiant sincerity, sparkling clarity and honeyed sweetness" mark the hymns of Ramalinga Swamigal.

रागः नाट

Raga: Nāṭa

1. मुन्नवने यानैमुखत्तवने मुत्तिनलं
चोन्नवने तूय्मेय्ञ्चुकन्तवने-मन्नवने
चिरपरने ऐङ्करने चेञ्जडैय ञ्चेकरने
तरपरने निन् ताळ् शरण्
उलकेलान्तऴैप्पवरु मदवरुवि
उऴुकुमा मुखमुं ऐङ्करमुं
इलकुचेम्मेनिक्काट्चियुं इरण्डोडु
इरण्डेन ओङ्कु तिण्डोळुन्
तिलकावाणुतलार् सिद्धि बुद्धिकळैच-
चेर्त्तणैत्तिडुं इरुमरुङ्कुं
विलकुऱा तेळियेन् विऴैन्तनन् सिद्धि
विनायक विघ्नेश्वरने।

munnavane yānaimukhattavane muttinalam
connavane tūymeyncukantavane mannavane
cirparane einkarane cenjḍaiyancekarane
tarparane nin tāḷ śaraṇ
ulakelāntazhaippavaru madavaruvi
uzhukumā mukhamum einkaramum
ilakucemmenikkāṭciyum iraṇḍoḍu
iraṇḍena onkutiṇḍoḷun
tilakāvāṇutalār siddhibuddhikaḷaic-
certtaṇaittiḍum irumarunkum
vilakurā taḷiyen vizhaintanan siddhi
vināyaka vighneśvarane.

1. Munnavane

O primal Lord! who are elephant faced!
Who teach the path to liberation!
Who are the embodiment of purity, truth and bliss!
O Lord of wisdom! O five-armed Lord! O Lord with matted hair! who take interest in your devotees!
I seek refuge in your feet!
You have a face, in which flows the ichor which can nourish the entire world!
You have five arms!
You manifest with a reddish body!
On your either side you have *Siddhi* and *Buddhi,* whom you embrace tightly!
O Siddhivinayaka, the embodiment of success, who have no leader above you, O *Vighnesvara,* remover of obstacles!
This lowly one venerates you totally!

राग: हंसध्वनि Raga: Hamsadhwani

2. नादमुङ्कटन्तु निऱैन्तु निन्मयमे
नानेन अऱिन्तु नान् तानाय्
भेदमुङ्कडन्त मौनराज्यत्तैप्
पेतैयेन् पिटिप्पतेन्नाळो?
एतमुञ्चमय वादमुं विडुत्तोर्
इतयमुं एऴैयेन् चिरमुं
वेदमुन्ताङ्कुं पादने सिद्धि
विनायक विघ्नेश्वरने।

nādamumkaṭantu niṛaintu ninmayame
nānena aṛintu nān tānāy
bhedamumkaḍantamaunarājyattaip
petaiyen piṭippetennāḷo?
etamuncamayavādamum viḍuttor
itayamum ezhaiyen ciramum
vedamuntānkum pādane siddhi
vināyaka vighneśvarane.

2. Nādamumkaṭantu

O Siddhi Vinayaka! O Vighnesvara!
O Lord who are the embodiment of success and have no leader above you! O Remover of obstacles!
When shall I, dumb as I am, attain that state of silence, which transcends sound and will be filled with your presence and in which I will realise myself, transcending differentiation?
Your feet bear the Vedas,
in them rest the hearts of ascetics and sages and the burden of this poor being that I am.

राग: सिन्धुभैरवि Raga: Sindhubhairavi

3. कानल्नीर् विऴैन्त मानेन वुलकक्
कट्टिनै नट्टुऴन्रलैयुं
ईन वञ्चक नेञ्चक पुलैयेनै
येन्ऱु कोण्डरुळ नाळुळदो ?
ऊनमोन्ऱिल्ला उत्तमरुळ्ळत्ते
ओङ्कु चीर्प्रणव वोळिये
वेनविल् करत्तोर्क्किनियवा सिद्धि
विनायक विघ्नेश्वरने।

kānalnīr vizhaintamānena vulakak
kaṭṭinai naṭṭuzhanralaiyum
īnavancaka nencakapulaiyenai
yenru koṇḍaruḷa nāḷuḷado?
ūnamonrillā uttamaruḷḷatte
onku cīrpraṇavavoḷiye
venavil karattorkkiniyavā siddhi
vināyaka vighneśvarane.

3. Kānal neer vizhainta

Does it take time to bless this pariah,
Who, like the deer fallen into the mirage, wanders about in this world,
sowing the seeds of bondage,
with a mind full of base treachery,
O Vighneswara! O Siddhi Vinayaka!
O Remover of obstacles!
O Embodiment of success, who have no leader above you?
O faultless, noble one!
who shine brilliantly in the heart!
O Radiance that is the Pranava sound, AUM!
Who are sweet to Subrahmania, the Lord who holds the spear!

राग: श्री Raga: Śrī

4. मुन्नरुन्तवत्तोन् मुर्कलन मुतला
मुनिवर्कळ् इनितु वीट्टैय
इन्नरुळ् पुरियु निन्नरुट् पेरुमै
इरविनुं पकलिनुं मरवेन्
एन्नरुं पोरुळे एन्नुयिर्क्कुयिरे
एन्नरशे! एनतुरवे
मन्नरु नेऱियिन् मन्निय वऱिवे
वल्लभैग्गणेश मामणिये।

munnaruntavatton murgalan mutalā
munivarkaḷ initu vīṭṭaiya
innaruḷ puriyu ninnaruṭperumai
iravinum pakalinum maṛaven
ennarum poruḷe ennuyirkkuyire
ennaraśe! enaturave
mannaru neṛiyin manniya vaṛive
vallabhaiggaṇeśamāmaṇiye.

4. Munnaruntavatton

O Ganesa, Lord of spiritual attendants!
O Lord of Vallabha!
O Jewel among elephants!
I shall not forget, day or night,
your gracious greatness,
in blessing sages like Mudgala, who did penance long ago,
You are my precious possession!
You are the Life of my life!
My ruler! my friend!
who shine as the guiding light in the righteousness of rulers.

रागः हिन्दोलं — Raga: Hindolam

5. तिरुवुङ्कल्वियुञ्चीरञ्चिऱप्पुमुन्
तिरुवटिप्पुकऴ् पाटुन्तिऱमुंनल्
उरुवुञ्चीलमुं उक्कमुन्ताऴवुऱ
उणर्वुन्तन्तेन तळ्ळत्तमंर्तवा।
गुरुवूं दैय्ववुमाकि अन्पाळर्तङ्
कुऱै तविर्क्कुङ्गुणप्पेरुङ्कुन्ऱमे
वेरुवुञ्चिन्तै विलकग्गजाननं
विळङ्कुम् सिद्धि विनायक वळ्ळले

tiruvumkalviyuncīrancirappumun
tiruvaṭippukazhpāṭuntiramum nal
uruvuncīlamum ūkkamuntāzhavur
uṇarvuntantena tuḷḷattamarntavā
guruvum deiyvavumāki anpāḷartang
kūrai tavirkkunguṇapperunkunrame
veruvuncintai vilaka ggajananam
viḷamkum siddhivināyaka vaḷḷale.

5. Tiruvumkalviyun

O Siddhi Vinayaka! O lord who are the embodiment of success!
Who have no leader above you!
O lord who have boundless generosity!
O lord who reside in my heart!
You bestow wealth, learning, various assets,
the capacity to sing the praises of your feet,
a good physical form, good character, perseverance, and humility!
Being God and teacher,
you destroy the deficiencies of your devotees!
You are a mountain of virtues!
To remove fear and worry, you shine with the elephant face!

रागः रीतिगौळ Raga: Rītigowḷa

6. शीतनाण् मलर् च्चेल्वनुमामलर्च्
चेल्विमार् पकच्चेल्वनुङ्काणकिलाप्
पाद नाटोरुप्पट्ट्रुरप्पट्टुवोर्
पाद नाडप्परिन्तरुळ् पालिप्पां
नाद नाडिय वन्तत्तिलोङ्कुमेय्ञ्
ज्ञान नाटक नायक नान्केनुं
वेद नाडिय मेय्प्पोरुळे यरुळ्
विळङ्कु सिद्धिविनायक वळ्ळले।

śītanāṇ malarccelvanumāmalarc
celvimāṛ pakaccelvanunkāṇakilāp
pāda nāṭoruppaṭṭrurappaṭṭruvor
pāda nāḍa pparintaruḷ pālippām
nāda nāḍiya vantattilonkumeyn
jnāna nāṭaka nāyaka nānkenum
veda nāḍiya meypporuḷe yaruḷ
viḷanku siddhivināyaka vaḷḷale.

6. Śeetanānmalar

O Siddhi Vinayaka!
O Lord who are the embodiment of success and have no leader above you!
O Lord with boundless generosity!
O True Being, on whom are based the four Vedas!
You have manifested yourself to bless!
You are the hero in the drama of true knowledge!
Please bless that:
in order to get rid of my bondages,
I should bow to the feet of those who have sought the feet of Lord Siva,
which could not be found either by
Brahma, the Lord who appeared in the lotus flower,
or by Visnu, on whose chest resides Lakshmi!

रागः देश | Raga: Deś

7. तञ्जमेन्ऱुनैच्चार्न्तन् नेन्तै नी
तानु मिन्तच्चकत्तवर् पोलवे
वञ्चमेन्नि इरुन्तिडिल् एन् चेय्वेन्?
वञ्चमट्र मनत्तुरै अण्णले
पञ्च पातकन् तीर्त्तनै एन्ऱु निन्
पादपङ्कजं पट्रिनन् पावियेन्
विञ्च नल्लरुळ् वेण्डित्तरुतियो
विळङ्कुम् सिद्धि विनायक वळ्ळले।

tanjamenrunai ccārntannentai nī
tānu mintaccakattavar polave
vanchamenni iruntiḍil en ceyven?
vancamaṭṭra manatturai aṇṇale
panca pātakan tīrttanai enru nin
pādapankajam paṭṭrinan pāviyen
vinca nallaruḷ veṇḍittarutiyo
vilankum siddhivināyaka vaḷḷale.

7. Tanjamenrunai

O Siddhi Vinayaka!
O Lord who are the embodiment of success and have no leader above you! O Lord with boundless generosity!
I seek refuge in you.
If, even you, like the people of this world,
do not play fair with me, what shall I do?
O Lord who reside in the hearts of those
who are devoid of falsehood and deceit,
The sinner that I am, sought your lotus-like feet,
in the hope that you would rid me of the five sins!

राग: शुद्धसावेरि Raga: Śuddhasāveri

8. कळ्ळनेञ्चकन् आयिनुं इय नान्
कळ्ळमिन्ऱि क्कऴुकिन्ऱेन् एनतु
उळ्ळ निन्ऱिरुवुळ्ळं अऱियुमे
ओतुकिन्ऱ तेन्पोतु कऴित्तिडेन्
वळ्ळ मामलर् प्पादप्पेरुं पुकऴ्
वाऴ्त्ति नात्तऴुं पेर् वऴङ्कुवाय्
वेळ्ळ वेणिप्पेरुन्तकैये अरुळ्
विळङ्कुं सिद्धिविनायक वळ्ळले।

kaḷḷanencakan āyinum iya nān
kaḷḷaminṛi kkazhrukinren enatu
uḷḷa ninriruvuḷḷam aṛiyume
otukinratenpotu kazhittiḍen
vaḷḷamāmalar ppādapperum pukazh
vāzhtti nāttazhumpera vazhankuvāy
veḷḷaveṇipperuntakaiye aruḷ
viḷankum siddhivināyaka vaḷḷale.

8. Kallanencakan

O Siddhi Vinayaka!
O Lord who are the embodiment of success and have no leader above You!
O Lord with boundless generosity!
who are ever there to bless me!
O Lord! Though I have a deceitful heart,
You know in your divine heart that now I am speaking without deceit!
O Lord with the moon on your head!
Bless me with a full life!
Bless me that I should go on singing your praises till my tongue gets seared!

रागः यमुनाकल्याणि | Raga: Yamunākalyāṇi

9. मण्णिलाशै मयक्कर् वेण्डिय
मातवर्क्कु मतिप्पुरियायुनै
एण्णिलार् चिरियेनै युमुन्निन्रे
येन्रु कोण्डनै इन्रु विटुत्तियो
उण्णि लाविय निन् तिरुवुळ्ळमुं
आशैयोडुवर्प्पङ्कोळ वेण्णुमो
वेण्णिला मुडियु पुण्णिय मूर्त्तिये
विळङ्कुम् सिद्धिविनायक वळ्ळले।

maṇṇilāśai mayakkaraveṇḍiya
mātavarkku matippuriyāyunai
eṇṇilārciriyenaiyumunninre
yenrukoṇḍanai inru viḍuttiyo
uṇṇilāviya nin tiruvuḷḷamum
āśaiyoḍuvarppankoḷa veṇṇumo
veṇṇilā muḍiyu puṇṇiya mūrttiye
viḷankum siddhivināyaka vaḷḷale.

9. Mannilāśai

O Siddhi Vinayaka!
O Lord who are the embodiment of success and have no leader above you!
O Lord with boundless generosity!
O Lord with the pure form, wearing the moon on your head!
O Lord who show the light of knowledge!
Even the sages who worship,
to get rid of their desires in this world,
cannot comprehend your greatness!
You have accepted me insignificant and lowly as I am!
Can you give me up now?
Can you show apathy to me?

राग: सुरुटि

Raga: Suruṭi

10. आणिलेयन्रि आरुयिर् पेण्णिले
अलियिले इव्वडियनै प्पोलवे
काणिलेन् ओरु पाविर्ये इप्पेरुङ्
कळ्ळ नेञ्च कक्कूटैयनै आळैया
एणिले यिडरेयृत विटुत्तियेल्
एन् चेय्केन् इनि इव्वुलकत्तिले
वीणिले युळैप्पेनरुळैयने
विळङ्कुं सिद्धि विनायक वळ्ळले।

āṇileyanri āruyirpeṇṇile
aliyile ivvaḍiyanaippolave
kāṇilen oru pārviye ipperung
kaḷḷa nencakakkaḍaiyanai āḷaiyā
eṇileyiḍareyta viḍuttiyel
en ceyken ini ivvulakattile
vīṇileyuzhaippenaruḷaiyane
viḷankum siddhivināyaka vaḷḷale.

10. Aṇileyanri

O Siddhi Vinayaka!
O Lord who are the embodiment of success and have no leader above you!
O Lord with boundless generosity!
You will not find a sinner like me among men, women or eunuchs!
Rule this sinner with an evil mind!
If you do not liberate me,
I shall toil in vain in this world!

रागः मध्यमावति Raga: Madhyamāvati

11. नाविनालुनै नाटोरुं पाटुवार्
नाडुवार् तमै नण्णि पुकऴ्वुं
ओय् विलातुनैप्पाटवुन्तुन्पेलां
ओडवुं मकिऴोङ्क वुञ्चेय्कुवाय्
काविनेर् कळत्तान् मकिऴ् ऐङ्करक्
कटवुळे नर्करुङ्कुऴि येन्नुमूर्
मेवियन् परक्करुळ् गणनाथने
विळङ्कुं सिद्धि विनायक वळ्ळले।

nāvinālunai nāṭorum pāṭuvār
nāḍuvār tamai naṇṇipukazhavum
oyvilātunaippāṭavuntunpelām
oḍavum makizhonkavunceykuvāy
kāvinerkaḷattān makizh einkarak
kaṭavuḷe narkarunkuzhiyennumūr
meviyanparakkaruḷ gaṇanāthane
viḷamkum siddhivināyaka vaḷḷale.

11. Nāvinalunai

O Siddhi Vinayaka!
O Lord who are the embodiment of success and have no leader above you!
O Lord with boundless generosity!
You drive away the distress and maximise the happiness of those who ceaselessly sing your praises!
O Five-armed Lord whom the blue-necked Lord Siva sees and rejoices!
O Elephant-faced Lord!
Bless this resident of Narkarunkuzhi!

HYMNS TO GAṆEŚA BY NILAKANTHA SIVAN

	Hymn	*Raga*
1.	Sri Ganapatiye tunai	Nata
2.	Vantenakkarul tantu	Kapi
3.	Gajanana Ganesvarane	Bandhuvarali

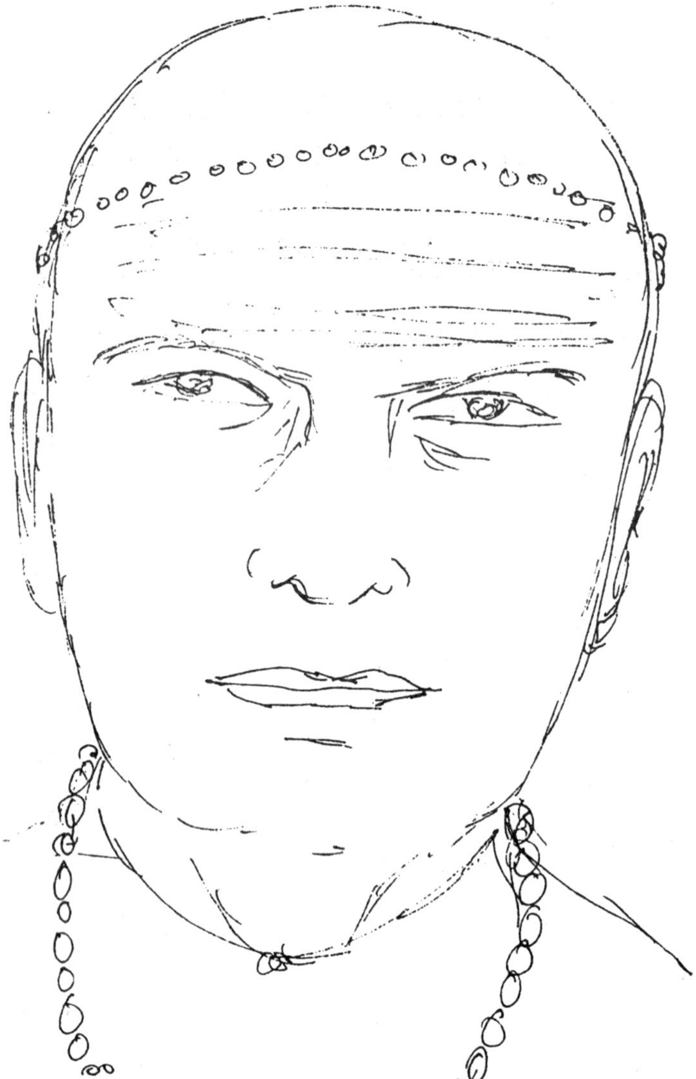

NILAKANTHA SIVAN

NILAKANTHA SIVAN (1839–1900 A.D.)

Nilakantha Sivan was a Saivite saint, who took to a life of prayer, devotion and music, resigning the job of Village Magistrate, which he held for 15 years.

He is believed to have performed miracles with the aid of his musical compositions.

Nilakantha Sivan mainly sang in Tamil, though there are a few Sanskrit songs as well.

The main refrain in his songs is an appeal to God to deliver from the worldly shackles of lust, anger, greed etc.

The hymns to Ganesa by Nilakantha Sivan included in this volume fully bear out this, as also his passionate devotion to God.

रागः नाटै

Raga: Nāṭai

1. श्री गणपतिये तुणै चेय्कुवाय् नीये
मोकमेकटन्तोङ्कुं परने
मुक्कण्णनीन्ऱ् मुतऱ् कुमरने
मा करुणै पेऱुमैङ्करने
मदवारण मामुख मातुमै बालक पावनने
देवर् मुनिवर् पोट्ट्रुं पादा तीयविनैकळ् माट्ट्रुं नाथा
नावलरेल्लां नम्पुं वेदा नान्मऱैप्पोता
पूवलंवर त्तातैयोतप्पुरकरन् वलंवन्तनीता।

śrī gaṇapatiye tuṇaiceykuvāy nīye
mokamekaṭantonkum parane
mukkaṇṇanīnramutarkumarane
mākaruṇaiperumainkarane
madavāraṇamāmukhamātumaibālaka pāvanane
devar munivar poṭṭrum pādā tīyavinaikaḷmāṭṭrum nāthā
nāvalarellām nampum vedā nānmaraippotā
pūvalamvara ttātaiyotappurakaran valamvantanītā.

1. Sri Ganapatiye Tunai

O auspicious Lord of spiritual attendants! Help me and bless me!
O supreme One, who shines transcending delusion, the first son of the three-eyed Lord Siva,
O five-armed Lord who shows great mercy!
O elephant-faced One, Son of Uma, the Divine Mother!
O pure Lord!
Your feet are worshipped by angels and sages!
O Lord who remove all evil and sin!
O Lord of wisdom in whom the poets trust implicitly,
You teach the four Vedas,
When your father asked you to go round the world, you went round the Lord who destroyed Tripura, Siva (your father)!

एवर् तुतियुं केट्कुं गाथा
एळि येन्ऱुति यीनुमुनक्किनिताय् ता वरदा
मायमिल्लात मऱैमुटिवे माकरुणैयेपेऱुं वटिवे
नीयेनक्केन्ऱुमुदवितरवे निनैप्पायिन् पुऱवे
आयुं वेण्पिऱै मुटिनि कऴ़वे यरुणीलकण्ठन् मनमकिऴ़वे
तूयवुनै मुन् पूजै चेय्यवे
तोडर् विनैयिडर् पकै केडवे सुन्दर सुखक्कर वुरुवे।

evartutiyum keṭkum gāthā
eḷiyenrutiyīnumunakkinitāy tā varadā
māyamillāta maraimuṭive mākaruṇaiyeperum vaṭive
nīyena kkenrumudavitarave ninaippāyin purave
āyum veṇpirai muṭini kazhave yarunīlakaṇṭhan manamakizhave
tūyavunai mun pūjaiceyyave
toḍar vinaiyiḍar pakaikeḍave sundara sukhakkara vuruve.

O Lord who listen to anyone's praise!
O granter of boons! Bless this lowly one with sweet blessings!
O Lord of Vedanta who are devoid of delusion!
O Lord who show great compassion!
You grant bliss to me, beyond my imagination!
You shine with the crescent moon on your crest,
the joy of the blue-necked Lord!
O pure One! If you are worshipped first,
all continuing evils and obstacles get destroyed!
O Lord who grant beautiful bliss!

राग: हिन्दुस्तानि कापि | Raga: Hindustāni Kāpi

2. वन्तेनक्कुरुळ्तन्तु मुन्निन्राळ् वक्रतुण्डा
अन्तनाळ् दशकन्धरन्रने पन्धेन वाटिय करने
अन्तर् पाडिय परने
विरिन्तुनन् मणञ्चिरन्तु मदनीर्
चोरिन्तु मत्तकत्तोड
विरैन्तु वन्तु मुन्रिरण्डतै युण्डु पुरण्डु वण्टुकळ् पाड
करङ्कळिर् पाशाङ्कुशमुं विळङ्क प्परन्तिरुकन्नमाड
करुम्पवल् पोरियरुन्ति यन्पक्र्कु पेरुङ्करुणैक्कुण् पोड
वरु ञ्चिवन्रिरुमैन्ता तिरुन्तनट्ट्रमिऴ्तन्ता
ळरुन्तवर्करुळ् चोन्ता शरण् चरणमोरुतन्ता।

vantenakkaruḷtantu munninrāḷ vakratuṇḍā
antanāḷ daśakandharanrane pandhenavāṭiyakarane
antar pāḍiya parane
virintunan maṇancirantumadanīr
corintu mattakattoḍa
viraintu vantu munriraṇḍatai yuṇḍu puraṇḍu vaṇṭukaḷ pāḍa
karamkaḷir pāśāmkuśamun viḷanka pparanti rukannamāḍa
karumpaval poriyarunti yanparkku perunkaru ṇaikkaṇ poḍa
varuncivanrirumaintā tiruntanaṭṭramizhtantā
ḷaruntavarkaruḷcontā śaraṇ caraṇamorutantā.

2. Vantenakkarul Tantu

O Lord with the curving trunk!
Come, bless me and appear before me and rule me!
Once long ago, you played, treating Ravana, the ten-headed demon like a ball!
O Lord eulogised by the angels!
Your broad temples ooze the fragrant ichor,
to which come fast the bees,
tasting which, intoxicated they sing (hum),
You shine with the noose and the goad in your hands,
the two broad cheeks dance,
after taking sugarcane juice and rice preparations,
you look at your devotees with compassionate eyes,
O holy son of Siva,
My own Lord! Come to bless me and remove my errors!
O Lord with the single tusk! you are my refuge, you are my refuge!

राग: बन्धुवराळि | Raga: Bandhuvarāḷi

3. गजानन गणेश्वरने करुणै चेय्वाय शरणं नीये
विशाल कर्ण वक्रतुण्ड वेलवनुक्कु
मून्रोनरिय मूलमुतप्पो रुळाकिय
फालचन्द्रवेणियन्पेट्ट्र बालावुमैलोला
पऴवकै पयरवतुण्डरुलुं शीलावनुकूला
नीलकण्ठ दासन् कविक्कु नेर्न्तुवन्तुरुळ् पोता
नित्तिय निर्मल निच्चल निष्कल सत्यसम्पत्प्रसादा
आलडितङ्कियदाता अन्पर् पणिन्तिडुं पादा
मालपनुं तोऴुं वेदा मङ्कळमरुळैङ्कर नाथा।

gajānana gaṇeśvarane karuṇai ceyvāy saraṇam nīye
viśālakarṇa vakratuṇḍa velavanukku
mūnronariya mūlamutapporuḷākiya
phālacandraveṇiyanpeṭṭrabālāvumailolā
pazhavakaipayaravatuṇḍarulumśīlāvanukūlā
nīlakaṇṭhadāsan kavikku nerntuvanturuḷ potā
nittiya nirmala niccala niṣkala satyasampatprasādā
ālaḍitankiyadātā anpar paṇintiḍum pādā
mālapanum tozhum vedā mankaḷamaruḷainkara nāthā.

3. Gajānana gaṇesvarane

O elephant-faced Lord! O Lord of spiritual attendants!
Be kind towards me. You are my only refuge!
You have wide ears, a curving trunk,
You are elder to Subrahmania, the Lord with the spear!
You are the primordial being the primal root!
You are the son born of the Lord with the moon on his forehead (Lord Siva) and the darling of *Uma*, the Divine Mother!
You are used to eat a variety of lentils and rice preparations!
You are always favourably inclined!
Can't you appear before this poet, *Nilakanthan* and bless him?
You are eternal, pure, immovable, stainless, truth personified,
You bestow all kinds of wealth!
You reside under the banyan tree, you giving Lord!
Your feet are worshipped by good ones!
O embodiment of knowledge who are worshipped even by Visnu,
O five-armed Lord! bless me with auspiciousness!

HYMNS TO GAṆEŚA BY NARAYANA GURU

	Hymn	*Raga*
1.	Namaddevabrindam	Hamsadhwani
2.	Kiladdevagotram	Nata
3.	Galaddahamalam	Sindhubhairavi
4.	Urastaraharam	Khamas
5.	Kararudhamoksham	Suruti
6.	Sadasam Suresam	Kharaharapriya
7.	Tatanekasantam	Mohanam
8.	Sivapremapindam	Madhyamavati

NARAYANA GURU

NARAYANA GURU (1856–1928 A.D.)

Though born as a low caste member of society, Narayana Guru attained the heights of spiritual greatness comparable to Sankara, the Nambudiri Brahmin.

He was a poet saint and composed several hymns in Sanskrit, a language in which he had great proficiency.

Narayana Guru's message was simple: "There is only one caste, only one religion and one God for man."

"Follow any religion, but become good and noble" was his exhortation.

The songs of Narayana Guru will be presented in volume eight of the Sacred Songs of India.

His hymns to Ganesa are only an illustrative precursor showing his devotion to God, poetic skill and proficiency in Sanskrit.

राग: हंसध्वनि | Raga: Hamsadhwani

1. नमद्देववृन्दं लसद्वेदकन्दं
शिरःश्रीमदिन्दुं श्रितश्रीमुकुन्दं
बृहच्चारुशुण्डं स्तुतश्री सनन्दं
जडाहीन्द्रकुन्दं भजे अभीष्टसन्दं।

namaddevavṛndam lasadvedakandam
śiraḥśrīmadindum śritaśrīmukundam
bṛhaccāruśuṇḍam stutaśrīsanandam
jaḍāhīndrakundam bhaje abhīṣṭasandam.

राग: नाटै | Raga: Nāṭai

2. किलद्देवगोत्रं कनद्धेमगात्रं
सदानन्दमात्रं महाभक्तमित्रं
शरत्चन्द्रवक्त्रं त्रयीपूतपात्रं
समस्तार्त्तिहात्रं भजे शक्तिपुत्रं।

kiladdevagotram kanaddhemagātram
sadānandamātram mahābhaktamitram
śaratcandravaktram trayīpūtapātram
samastārttihātram bhaje śaktiputram.

1. Namaddevavrindam

I worship that Lord
to whom groups of angels bow,
who shines as the root of the Vedas,
who has the moon on the head,
who is venerated by the auspicious Visnu (Mukunda),
who has a big and beautiful trunk,
who is eulogised by Brahma,
who is offered the jasmine flowers by Siva and Indra
and who fulfils desires.

2. Kiladdevagotram

I bow to the son of Sakti, the Divine Mother,
who is of divine lineage,
whose body is like gold,
who is ever blissful,
who is the great friend of devotees,
whose face is like autumnal moon,
who has been rendered pure thrice,
who destroys all afflictions!

राग: सिन्धुभैरवि

Raga: Sindhubhairavi

3. गळद्दानमालं चलद्भोगिमालं
गळाम्बोदकालं सदा दानशीलं
सुरारातिकालं महेशात्मबालं
लसत् पुण्ड्रफालं भजे लोकमूलं।

galaddānamālam caladbhogimālam
galāmbodakālam sadā dānaśīlam
surārātikālam maheśātmabālam
lasatpuṇḍraphālam bhaje lokamūlam.

राग: खमाज़

Raga: Khamās

4. उरस्तारहारं शरत्चन्द्रहीरं
सुरश्री विचारं हृतार्त्तारिभारं
कडे दानपूरं जडाभोगिपूरं
कलाबिन्दुतारं भजे शैववीरं।

urastārahāram śaratcandrahīram
suraśrīvicāram hṛdārttāribhāram
kaḍe dānapūram jaḍābhogipūram
kalābindutāram bhaje śaivavīram.

3. Galaddānamālam

I worship the root of the world,
who wears a garland round his neck,
who wears moving snakes as a garland,
whose neck is dark as a cloud,
who is ever inclined to bestow gifts,
who is death to the enemies of angels,
the son of the great Lord, Siva,
on whose forehead shines the sandal mark.

4. Urastārahāram

I worship the heroic son of Siva,
on whose chest the necklace flourishes like a star,
with pearls resembling the autumnal moon,
who is the auspicious object of thought for celestials,
who destroys the burden of afflictions,
who gives gifts even to the dumb,
whose head is full of snakes,
who is the shining star of *kala* and *bindu*.*

**Kala* and *Bindu* are centres of creation.

राग: सुरुटि | Raga: Suruṭi

5. करारूढमोक्षं विपद्भङ्गदक्षं
चलत्सारसाक्षं पराशक्तिपक्षं
श्रितामर्त्यवृक्षं सुरारि द्रुतक्षं
परानन्दपक्षं भजे श्रीशिवाक्षं।

karārūḍhamokṣam vipadbhangadakṣam
calatsārasākṣam parāśaktipakṣam
śritāmartyavṛkṣam surāridrutakṣam
parānandapakṣam bhaje śrīśivākṣam.

राग: खरहरप्रिय | Raga: Kharaharapriya

6. सदाशं सुरेशं सदा पातुमीशं
निदानोद्भवं शाङ्कर प्रेम कोशं
धृतश्रीनिशेशं लसद्दन्तकोशं
चलच्छुलपाशं भजे कृत्तपाशं।

sadāśam sureśam sadā pātumīśam
nidānodbhavam śānkarapremakośam
dhṛtaśrīniśeśam lasaddantakośam
calacchūlapāśam bhaje kṛttapāśam.

5. Karārūḍhamokśam

I worship the auspicious eye of Siva,
who has liberation ready to be granted in his hand,
who is competent in breaking up dangers,
who is the true witness of all that happens,
who sides with the supreme power, the Divine Mother,
who is worshipped by the immortal angels,
who is clever in destroying the enemies of angels,
who is ever on the side of supreme bliss.

6. Sadāśam Sureśam

I worship the Lord who has cut off attachment,
who is ever full of hope,
the Lord of angels,
the Lord who is ever ready to protect,
who is the cause of creation,
who is the love treasure of Siva,
who wears the auspicious moon,
whose tusk shines,
who holds the trident and the noose.

रागः मोहनं | Raga: Mohanam

7. ततानेकसन्तं सदा दानवन्तं
बुधश्रीकरन्तं गजास्यं विभान्तं
करात्मीयदन्तं त्रिलोकैकवृन्दं
सुमन्दं परन्तं भजेऽहं भवन्तं।

tatānekasantam sadā dānavantam
budhaśrīkarantam gajāsyam vibhāntam
karātmīyadantam trilokaikavṛndam
sumandam parantam bhajeham bhavantam.

रागः मध्यमावति | Raga: Madhyamāvati

8. शिवप्रेमपिण्डं परं स्वर्णवर्णं
लसद्दन्तखण्डं सदानन्दपूर्णं
विवर्णप्रभाण्डं धृतस्वर्णभाण्डं
चलच्चारुशुण्डं भजे दन्तितुण्डं।

śivapremapiṇḍam param svarṇavarṇam
lasaddantakhaṇḍam sadānandapūrṇam
vivarṇaprabhāṇḍam dhṛtasvarṇabhāṇḍam
calaccāruśuṇḍam bhaje dantituṇḍam.

7. Tatānekasantam

I worship the creator,
who exists in many forms,
who is ever generous in giving,
whose hands give knowledge and prosperity,
who shines with the elephant face,
who holds his own tusk in hand,
the unique one venerated by the three worlds,
who is of good intellect and is the supreme goal.

8. Sivapremapiṇḍam

I worship the elephant-faced Lord,
who is the manifestation of Siva's love,
the supreme one, who is golden-hued,
who shines with the broken piece of tusk,
who is always full of bliss,
who shines in diverse colours,
who wears a lot of gold on his body,
who has a beautiful, moving trunk.

HYMNS TO GAṆEŚA BY SWAMI BRAHMANANDA

	Hymn	*Raga*
1.	Jaya Ganesa Gananatha	Peelu
2.	Prathama Sumar Sri Ganesa	Darbari Kanada

SWAMI BRAHMANANDA

SWAMI BRAHMANANDA (1863–1922 A.D.)

Swami Brahmananda was a disciple of Ramakrishna Paramahamsa.

He considered Swami Vivekananda as his elder brother.

As a true disciple of Ramakrishna Paramahamsa, Swami Brahmananda attained the same level of spirituality and higher state of consciousness that Ramakrishna reached.

The two hymns to Ganesa composed by Swami Brahmananda included in this volume illustrate his childlike simplicity, which is the mark of all great saints.

राग: पीलु | Raga: Peelu

1. जय गणेश गणनाथ दयानिधे
सकल विघ्न कर दूर हमारे
प्रथम धरे जो ध्यान तुम्हारे
जिसके पूरण कारज सारे
लम्बोदर गजवदन मनोहर
कर त्रिशूल परशु वर धारे।

jaya gaṇeśa gaṇanātha dayānidhe
sakal vighna kar dūr hamāre
prathama dhare jo dhyān tumhāre
jiske pūraṇ kāraj sāre
lambodar gajavadan manohar
kar triśūl paraśu var dhāre.

ऋद्धि सिद्धि दोउ चमर डुलावे
मूषक वाहन परम सुकारे
ब्रह्मादिक सुर ध्यावत मनमें
ऋषि मुनिगण सब दास तुम्हारे
ब्रह्मानन्द सहाय करो नित
भक्तजनों के तुं रखवारे।

riddhi siddhi dou camar ḍulāve
mūṣakavāhana param sukāre
brahmādik sur dhyāvat manmen
rishimunigaṇa sab dās tumhāre
brahmānand sahāy karo nit
bhakta janom ke tum rakhvāre.

1. Jaya Ganesa Gananātha

Hail! *Ganesa*! *Gananatha*! Lord of spiritual attendants!
O Treasurehouse of compassion!
Remove all our obstacles far away!
He who meditates first on you,
has all his tasks completed (successfully).
O big bellied, elephant-faced handsome Lord!
who hold the trident, axe and boons in your hands!

Let *riddhi* and *Siddhi** both fan you!
O supreme Lord, who ride the mouse and do good things!
Celestials like Brahma and others meditate in their mind on you!
Sages and saints are all your servants!
Daily help this Brahmanand!
You are the Protector of your devotees!

**Riddhi* is prosperity and *Siddhi* is achievement or success.

राग: दरबारि कानडा

Raga: Darbāri Kānaḍā

2. प्रथम सुमर श्री गणेश
गौरीसुत प्रिय महेश
सकल विघ्न भय क्लेश
दूर से निवारे
लम्बोदर भुज विशाल
कर त्रिशूल सुन्दर बाल
शोभत गल पुष्पमाल
रक्त वसन धारे।

pratham sumar śrī gaṇeś
gaurīsut priya maheś
sakalavighnabhay kleś
dūrse nivāre
lambodar bhuj viśāl
kar triśūl sundar bāl
śobhat gal puṣpamāl
raktavasan dhāre.

2. Prathama Sumar Śrī Gaṇeśa

First remember auspicious Ganesa!
Son of *Gauri,* the fair goddess!
the darling great Lord!
Remove far away all the fears and afflictions of obstacles!
O big bellied Lord with strong and long arms!
O handsome boyish Lord who hold the trident in your hand!
You wear on your neck an auspicious garland of flowers and a red garment.

ऋद्धि सिद्धि दोउ नार
चमर करत बार बार
मूषक वाहन सवार
भक्तन हितकारी
पूर्ण गुण गण निदान
सुरमुनि यश करत गान
ब्रह्मानन्द चरण ध्यान
सकल काज सारे।

riddhi siddhi dou nār
camar karat bār bār
mūṣak vāhan savār
bhaktan hitkārī
pūrṇaguṇ gaṇ nidān
suramuniyaś karat gān
brahmānand caraṇ dhyān
sakal kāj sāre.

The two ladies Riddhi and Siddhi fan you again and again!
You ride the mouse!
You do what is good for your devotees!
You are the abode of all the good qualities!
Angels and sages sing of your glory!
Brahmanand meditates on your feet!
Complete all my tasks!

HYMN TO GAṆEŚA BY HARIKESANALLUR MUTHIAH BHAGAVATAR

	Hymn	*Raga*
1.	Siddhi Vinayakam	Mohanakalyani

HARIKESANALLUR MUTHIAH BHAGAVATAR

HARIKESANALLUR MUTHIAH BHAGAVATAR (1877–1945 A.D.)

Harikesanallur Muthiah Bhagavatar was one of the outstanding music composers of South India, in the post Trinity period. He followed in the trail blazed by Tyagaraja, Muttuswami. Dikshitar and Syama Sastri.

Nādopāsanā or music as a means of devotion to attain spiritual heights is a well accepted path.

Muthiah Bhagavatar's skill in composing new and rare musical melodies or Ragas and his deep knowledge of Puranic lore enabled him to compose beautiful songs in praise of various deities listening to which one could go into spiritual ecstasy.

The songs of Muthiah Bhagavatar will be included in a subsequent volume of the Sacred Songs of India.

The hymn to Ganesa, in the Raga Mohanakalyani, included in this volume will show what magic Muthiah Bhagavatar can work with his musical compositions.

रागः मोहनकल्याणि Raga: Mohanakalyāṇi

1. सिद्धिविनायकं सेवेऽहं वरं
बुद्धिदेवीवरं भोगिकङ्कणवरं
शुद्धकलेबरं सोम कलाधरं
मोदक हस्तं मूषिकवाहं
मुनिहृद्येकं मोहनिदानं
वेद समूहं बोध प्रवाहं
श्रीधनि वासं शृतहरि केशं।

siddhivināyakam seve aham varam
buddhidevīvaram bhogikankaṇavaram
suddhakalebaram somakalādharam
modakahastam mūṣikavāham
munihṛdyekam mohanidānam
vedasamūham bodhapravāham
śrīdhanivāsam śṛtaharikeśam.

1. Siddhivinayakam seve aham

   I worship the great *Siddhi Vinayaka*, the embodiment of success, who has no leader above him,
   who is the spouse of Buddhi devi, the goddess of intellect,
   who has the snake for his bangle,
   who has a pure body,
   who wears a digit of the moon,
   who holds the rice cake in his hand,
   who rides the mouse,
   the only one who resides in the hearts of sages,
   who destroys delusion,
   who is in the cluster of Vedas,
   who makes wisdom flow,
   who resides in auspicious prosperity,
   and who is worshipped by Harikesa.

HYMNS TO GAṆEŚA BY SUBRAMANIA BHARATI

	Hymn	*Raga*
1.	Karpaga Vināyaka Kadavule	Nata
2.	Vidhiye Vāzhi Vināyaka Vāzhi	Hamsadhwani
3.	Ennai nī Kappai	Kamboji
4.	Kadamai Yavanai	Sindhubhairavi

SUBRAMANIA BHARATI

SUBRAMANIA BHARATI
(11 December 1882–12 September 1921 A.D.)

Subramania Bharati, the doyen of Tamil poets, was a philosopher, besides being an ardent patriot of the pre-Independence era in India. Though he lived only a short life of 39 years, his poetic output was prodigious.

Subramania Bharati was a deeply religious person, though he did not believe in orthodoxy and rigidities of caste distinctions.

He believed in the brotherhood of mankind and considered God as the Supreme Power manifesting as and guiding the universe. Though he was an advaitin at heart, he also believed in the various manifestations of Divinity as Krishna, Muruga, Ganesa, Devi or Sakti etc.

His devotional songs are a veritable granary of devotion and spirituality.

रागः नाट

Raga: Nāṭa

1. कर्पग विनायकक्कडवुळे, पोट्रि
चिऱ्पर मोनत्तेवन् वाऴ्ग
वारण मुखत्तान् मलर्त्तळ् वेल्ग
आरण मुखत्तान् अरुट्पदं वेलग
पडैप्पुक् किऱैयवन् पण्णवर् नायकन्
इन्दिर गुरु येनदियत्तोळिर्वन्
चन्दरमौलित्तलैवन् मैन्दन्

karpaga vināyakakkaḍavuḷé poṭṛi
ciṛpara monattavan vālzhga
vāraṇa mukhattān malarttāḷ velga
ārana mukhattān arutpadam velga
paḍaippukkiṛaiyavan paṇṇavar nāyakan
indira guru yenadiyattoḷirvān
chandira moulittalaivan maindan

गणपति ताळै क्करुत्तिडै वैप्पोम्;
गुणमदिर्पलवां; कूरक्केलीर्;
उट्चेवि त्तिरक्कुं; अगक्कण् ओळितरुम्;
अग्नि तोन्रुं; आण्मै वलियुरुम्;

Gaṇapati tāḷaikkaruttiḍai vaippom;
guṇamadiṛ palavām; kūṛakkéḷīr;
uṭcévi tiṛakkum; agakkaṇ oḷi tarum;
agni tonṛum; āṇmai valiyuṛum;

1. Karpaga Vinayaka

O! Lord Karpaga Vinayaka! Salutations!
O! Lord of great beauty! Hail!
Let the lotus feet of the Elephant-faced One be victorious!
Let the gracious step of the mouthpiece of the Vedas be victorious!
He is the Lord of creation! the Chief of litterateurs!
He is Indra's teacher! who gives radiance to my heart!
He is the son of the crescent-crested Lord!

Let us keep the feet of Ganapati in our thoughts!
There are many benefits in this, please listen!
The inner ears will open, inner eye will give light!
Fire will appear! Manliness will increase!

दिक्केलां वेन्रु जयक्कोडि नाट्टलाम्
कट् चेवि तन्नै क्कैयिले येडुक्कलाम्;
विडत्तैयुं नोवैयुं वेंपकैयदनैयुम्
तुच्चमेन्रेण्णि त्तुयरिलादिंगु
निच्चलुं वाऴ्न्दु निलैपेट्रोगंलाम्;
अच्चन् तीरुं; अमुदं विळैयुम्;
वित्तै वळरुं; वेळ्वि योङ्गुम्;
अमरत्तन्मैयु मेय्दवुम्
इङ्गु नां पेरलां; इह्दुणर्वीरे।।

dikkelām venru jayakkoḍi nāṭṭalām
kaṭcevi tannaik kaiyilé yeḍukkalām;
viḍattaiyum novaiyum vempakaiyadanaiyum
tucca menṛeṇṇit tuya rilādingu
niccalum vāzhndu nilaipeṭrongalām;
accan tīrum; amudam viḷaiyum;
vittai vaḷarum; veḷviyongum;
amarattanmaiyu meidavum
ingu nām peṛalām; ihduṇarvīre.

We can plant the flag of victory everywhere!

We can safely handle snakes!

Treating poison, disease and enmity as trifles, we can live without sorrow and flourish!

Fear will end, immortality will prevail!

Learning will grow!

Penances and sacrifices will flourish!

We can achieve here and now Truth and immortality!

Let us realise this!

राग: हंसध्वनि

Raga: Hamsadhwani

2. विधिये वाऴि विनायका वाऴि
पतिये वाऴि परमा वाऴि
चितैविनै नीक्कुं दैयूवमे पोट्ट्रि
पतुविनै काट्टुं पुण्णिया पोट्ट्रि
मतियिनै वळर्क्कूमन्ने पोट्ट्रि
इच्छैयुं विरियैयु ज्ञानमु मेन्राक्कु
मूलशक्तियिन् मुतलूवा पोट्ट्रि
पिरैमति चूडिय पेरुमान् वाऴि
निरैविनै चेक्कु निर्मलन् वाऴि
कालमून्रैयुङ्कटन्तान् वाऴि।।

vidhiye vāzhi vināyakā vāzhi
patiye vāzhi paramā vāzhi
citaivinai nīkkum deivame poṭṭri
patuvinai kāṭṭum puṇṇiyā poṭṭri
matiyinai vaḷarkkamanne poṭṭri
icchaiyumviriyaiyujnānamumenrārkku
mūlaśaktiyin mutalvā poṭṭri
piraimati cūḍiya perumān vāzhi
niraivinai cerkku nirmalan vāzhi
kālamūnraiyumkaṭantān vāzhi.

2. Vidhiye Vāzhi

O Creator! Salutations!
O Lord who have no leader above you! Salutations!
O Master! O Supreme One! Salutations!
O God who remove evil from the mind! Prostrations!
O Pure One, who show the right action! Prostrations!
To ennoble desire, action and knowledge,
O eldest son of primal power, the Divine Mother! Prostrations!
Hail! O Lord who wear the crescent moon! Hail!
O pure Lord who grant total fullness! Hail!
O Lord who transcend the three periods of time (past, present and future)! Salutations!

शक्तिदेवि चरणं वाऴि
वेट्ट्रि वाऴि वीरं वाऴि
भक्ति वाऴि पलपल कालमुं
उण्मै वाऴि ऊक्कं वाऴि
नल्ल गुणङ्कळे नम्मिदै यमरर्
पदङ्कळां कण्डीर् पारिडै मक्कळे
कृतयुगत्तिनै केडिन्रि निरुत्त
विरतनान् कोण्डनन् वेट्ट्रि
तरुम्शुडर् विनायकन् ताळिणै वाऴिये।।

śaktidevi caraṇam vāzhi
veṭṭri vāzhi vīram vāzhi
bhakti vāzhi palapala kālamum
uṇmai vāzhi ūkkam vāzhi
nalla guṇankaḷe nammidaiyamarar
padankaḷām kaṇḍīr pāriḍaimakkaḷe
kṛtayugattinai keḍinri nirutta
viratanān koṇḍanan veṭṭri
tarumcuḍar vināyakan tāḷiṇai vāzhiye.

Salutations to the feet of *Sakti*, the Divine Mother!
Long live: victory, valour!
Long live: devotion!
Let truth prevail for many many years, as also strength!
O people of the world!
Good qualities are the feet of angels in us!
I have taken a vow to establish *Krita Yuga** in this land!
Salutations to the feet of the effulgent Lord *Vinayaka*, the Lord who has no leader above him and who will give us victory!

---

*According to Hinduism, there are four yugas in the Time cycle. These yugas (or periods) are:

1. Krita (or Satya) Yuga (1.728 million years),

2. Treta Yuga (1.296 million years),

3. Dvapara Yuga (864000 years) and

4. Kali Yuga (432000 years).

Of these Krita Yuga was the golden age, when unity and righteousness prevailed.

Subramania Bharati, hence, means he has taken a vow to establish the golden age in his land.

रागः काम्बोजि

Raga: Kāmboji

3. एन्न नी काप्पाय् यावुमान् देय्वमे
पोऱ्त्तारन्ऱे पूमियाल्वार्
यावुनी यायि ननैत्तैयुं पोऱ्त्तल्
चेव्विय नेऱियतिर् शिवनिलै पेऱलां
पोङ्कुतल् पोक्किप्पाऱैयेनक्कीवाय्
मङ्गल गुणपति मणक्कुळक् गणपति
नेञ्चक्कमलत्तु निऱैन्तरुळ् पुरिवाय्
अकल् विऴियुमै याळाशैमकने॥

enna nī kāppāy yāvumān deivame
poruttāranre pūmiyālvār
yāvuni yāyi nanaittaiyum poruttal
cevviya neriyatir śivanilai peralām
ponkutal pokki pporaiyenkkīvāy
mangala guṇapati maṇakkuḷakgaṇapati
nencakkamalattu niraintaruḷ purivāy
akal vizhiyumaiyāḷāśaimakane.

3. Ennai nee kāppai

O God who are everything! You should protect me!

Only the patient can rule the world!

Because you are everything, you tolerate everything!

By following the righteous path of patience one can attain Divine status!

Remove tumult and give me serenity,

O auspicious *Ganapati,* Lord of spiritual attendants!

O *Ganapati* who reside in *Manikkulam*!*

Bless me filling the lotus of my heart!

O son of the large eyed *Uma,* the Divine Mother!

*Subramania Bharati was a devotee of the Deity in Manikkulam temple, Ganesa.

Though God is omnipresent and immanent, mystic poets have poured out their devotion to specific deities in specific temples. Subramania Bharati was no exception.

नाट्रिनै त्तुयरिन्रि नन्कमै त्तिडुवतुं
उळमेनु नाट्टै योरु पिऴै यिन्रि
आळ्वतुं पेरोळि ज्ञायिरे यनैय
चुडर् तरु मतियोडु तुयरिन्रि वाऴ्तलुं
नोक्कमा क्कोण्डु निन्पद नोक्किनेन्
कात्तरुळ् पुरिक कर्पक विनायका
कात्तरुळ् पुरिक कटवुळे युलकेल्लां
कोत्तरुळ् पुरिक कुरिप्परुं पोरुळे
अङ्कुश पाशमुङ् कोम्पुन् धरित्ताय्
एङ्कुल देवा पोट्रि
शंकरन् मकने ताळिणै पोट्रि।।

nāṭṭinai ttuyarinri nankamaittiḍuvatum
uḷamenu nāṭṭai yorupizhaiyinri
āḷvatum peroḷi jnāyireyanaiya
cuḍartarumatiyoḍu tuyarinri vāzhtalum
nokkamākkoṇḍu nin pada nokkinen
kāttaruḷ purika karpakavināyakā
kāttaruḷpurika kaṭavuḷe yulakellām
kottaruḷpurika kuripparum poruḷe
ankuśapāśamungkompun dharittāy
enkuladevā poṭṭri
śankaranmakane tāḷiṇai poṭṭri.

I looked at your feet,
with the object of ensuring that the land that is our mind
should be ruled without distress
and we should live a life of knowledge,
radiant like the rays of the sun,
and all should live without sorrow!

O *Karpaka Vinayaka*!

O wish granting Lord, who have no leader above you!
Protect and bless!

Protect and bless O God!

Bless that the world be united as one!

O dear Lord! who hold the noose, goad and the tusk!

Lord of my lineage! Salutations!

O Son of Sankara, Creator of bliss! Salutations!

राग: सिन्धुभैरवि　　　　Raga: Sindhubhairavi

4. कटमै यावन तन्नै कट्टुतल्
पिऱर् तुयर् तीर्त्तल् पिऱर् नलं वेण्डुतल्
विनायक देवनाय् वेलुटै कुमरनाय्
नारायणनाय नदिच्चडैमुटियनाय्
पिऱनाट्टिरुप्पोर् पेयर्पल कूऱि
अल्ला येहोवा एन त्तोळु तन्पुरुं
देवरुन्तानाय् तिरुमकल् भारति
उमैयेनुं देविय रुकन्तवान् पोरुळाय्
उलकेलाङ्काक्कुमोरुवनै प्पोट्टुतल्
इन्तान् केयिप्पूमियिलेवर्क्कुं
कटमै येनप्पडुं पयनितिल् नान्कां
अऱं पोरुळ् इन्पं वीटेनु मुरैये
तन्नैयाळुञ्चमर्त्तेनक्करुळ्वाय्।।

kaṭamai yāvana tannai kaṭṭutal
pirar tuyartīrttal pirar nalam venḍutal
vināyakadevanāy veluṭaikumaranāy
nārāyaṇanāy nadiccaḍaimuṭiyanāy
piranāṭṭiruppor peyar pala kūri
allā yehovā ena ttozhutanpuram
devaruntānāy tirumakal bhārati
umaiyenum deviyarukantavān poruḷāy
ulakelāmkākkumoruvanai ppoṭṭrutal
intān keyippumiyilevarkkum
kaṭamai yenappaḍum, payanitil nānkām
aṛam, poruḷ, inpam, vīṭenu muraiye
tannaiyāḷuncamarttenakkaruḷvāy.

4. Kadamai yãvana

Having control over oneself,
removing others' misery,
desiring others' good,
Bowing to one God,
Bowing to one God,
whether He is called:
Vinayaka, or as Kumara (Subrahmania),
the Lord with the spear,
or as Narayana (Visnu),
or as Siva, the Lord who bears the river (Ganga) in his matted hair,
or as various names mentioned in foreign countries:
like Allah, Yehova etc,
or as Lakshmi, Sarasvati or Uma,
This is the duty of everyone in this world!
The beneficial results are fourfold:
Dharma, Artha, Kama and Moksha, the four goals which guide our life!
Bless us accordingly!

मणकुळ विनायका वान्मरैत्तलैवा
तनैत्तानाळुं तन्मैतान् पेट्ट्रिटिल्
एल्ला प्पयन्कळुन्तामे येय्तुं
अशैया नेश्च मरुळ्वाय् उयिरेल्लां
इन्पुट्ट्रिरुक्क वेण्डि निन् निरुनाळ्
पणिवते तोऴिलेनक्कोण्डु
गणपति देवा, वाऴ्वेन् कळित्ते।।

maṇakuḷa vināyakā, vānmaraittalaivā
tanaittānāḷum tanmaitān peṭṭriṭil
ellā ppayankaḷuntāme yeytum
aśaiyā nencamaruḷvāy, uyirellām
inpuṭṭrirukka veṇḍi ninnirunāḷ
paṇivate tozhilenakkoṇḍu
gaṇapati devā, vāzhven kaḷitte.

O Vinayaka, Lord who have no Leader above you,
who reside in Manakkulam!

O Leader! O Lord, who are the essence of the Vedas!

If I can acquire the capacity to control myself,
I will attain all results desired,

Bless me with an unflinching heart!

I would like all living beings to be happy,
It is for this that I bow at your two feet!

O Lord Ganapati! Lord of spiritual attendants!

I shall live happily with your grace!

HYMNS TO GAṆEŚA BY PAPANASAM SIVAN

	Hymn	*Raga*
1.	Mūladharamurti	Hamsadhwani
2.	Sri Vatapi Ganapatiye	Sahana
3.	Tarunamidayya	Sivaranjani
4.	Tatvamariya tarama	Ritigowla
5.	Gajavadana karunasadana	Sri Ranjani
6.	Sri Ganapatiye	Devamanohari
7.	Ganapatiye Karunanidhiye	Kharaharapriya
8.	Vighnavinayakamurtikku mangalam	Madhyamavati

PAPANASAM SIVAN

PAPANASAM SIVAN (26 September 1890–1 October 1973 A.D.)

Papanasam Sivan, the Tamil music composer, has been termed "Tamil Tyagaraja".

His musical compositions, mainly in Tamil and numbering over 2000, are surcharged with devotion to God in His various manifestations.

He was born in Polagam village in Thanjavur district.

His original name was Ramaiah, and in many of his songs, he has inserted his pen-name as "Ramadasa". But because he lived for some time in Papanasam and was attired like a Saivite devotee, wearing *rudraksha* and holy ashes, he came to be known as "Papanasam Sivan".

Sivan was fond of conducting Bhajans and visited the various temples of Tamil Nadu, singing soul-stirring songs.

From 1930, he started living in Mylapore Madras. He was specially attached to the Lord in the Kapali temple and many of his most heart-rending devotional songs centre around the Deities in this temple: *Lord Kapali* and *Mother Karpagam*.

Sivan lived upto the age of 83 years and kept himself busy composing and singing the glories of his beloved Deities. He freely mixed Sanskrit with Tamil in his songs, which are a perfect combination of *Bhakti, Rāga, Sangeeta* and *Sāhitya*.

राग: हंसध्वनि

Raga: Hamsadhwani

1. मूलाधार मूर्त्ति ग़जमुखने शरणं उनदु उभय शरणम्
वेलायुध गुहन् तनक्कु मुन् तोन्रिय
विमला उमैयाळ् तरु मकने
अमला येमैयाळ् मुनिवर् तोऴुम्
अन्पुडन् तुम्बै यरुगं पुल्लै येडुत्
तरुच्चनै चेय्दालुं पोदुम्-अन्बर्
तुन्पं तुडैत्तुप्पेरिन्बम् तरुं वरदा
तुणै पुरि प्रणवाकार गणपतिये।।

mūlādhara mūrtti gajamukhané śaraṇam
unadu ubhaya śaraṇam
vélāyudha guhan tanakku mun tonriya
vimalā umaiyāḷ taru makané
amalā yemaiyāḷ munivar tozhum
anpuḍan tumbai yarugam pullai yéḍut
taruccanai ceydālum podum-anbar
tunpam tuḍaittuppérinbam tarum varadā
tuṇai puri praṇavākāra gaṇapatiyé.

1. Muladhaara Murti

O! Elephant-faced One! embodied in Moolaadhara!
I seek refuge in you again and again.
Born before Guha, the holder of the spear.
You are the Holy son of Uma, the stainless One!
The pure minded sages bow to you!
Even if worshipped with *Tumbai* and *arugam* grass* but with love
You remove sorrow and bestow bliss! O! Granter of boons!
Help me O! Ganapati! who is in the form of Pranava (Aum).
O! Elephant-faced One! embodied in Mooladhara!
I seek refuge in you.

*Easily available weeds.

राग: सहाना Raga: Sahānā

2. श्री वातापि गणपतिये निन् तिरुवटिये शरणं
देवादिदेवन् त्यागेशन् तिरुविळैयाडल् चेय् तिरुवारुर् वळर्
नम्पिन्पेर् इहपरं इरण्डिलुं नल् वाऴ्वुं पेरिन्पमुं नल्कुं
तुम्पिऴक पेरुमाळे अटि तोऴुं तोण्डर्कळ् वेण्डुंवरं तरुवोने
शम्भुवुटन् कमलाम्बिकै मकिऴुं तनयने दयापरने जगं पुकऴुं
कुम्भ मुनिनक्करुळ् कुमरमुन् तोन्रिय गोमाने रामदासन् उळंवळर्।।

śrī vātāpi gaṇapatiye nin tiruvaṭiye śaraṇam
devādidevan tyāgeśantiruviḷaiyāḍalcey tiruvārurvaḷar
nampinper ihaparam iraṇḍilum nal vāzhvum perinpamum nalkum
tumpizhaka perumāḷe aṭi tozhum toṇḍarkaḷ veṇḍum varam taruvone
śambhuvuṭan kamalāmbikai makizhum tanayane dayāparane jagam pukazhum
kumbhamuninakkaruḷ kumaramuntonriya gomāne rāmadāsan uḷamvaḷar.

2. Sri Vatahi Ganapatiye

O auspicions Vatapi Ganapati!
Your holy feet are my refuge!
You are the Lord of angels!
You are Tyagesa, the Lord who is the embodiment of sacrifice!
O Lord who reside in Tiruvaarur! manifest your auspicious sporting actions!
To those who trust in you, you bestow good life and bliss here and the hereafter!
O Lord whose trunk is a hand, who grant the boons sought by devotees who bow at your feet!
O son who delight Sambhu, the Creator of bliss and *Kamalambika*, the Divine Mother,
O compassionate One, who blessed the famous Agastya,
and appeared before Subrahmania
Gladden the heart of Ramadasa!

राग: शिवरञ्जनि

Raga: Śivaranjani

3. तरुणमिदैया दयै पुरि तुतिक्कैया उरिय
शरणं एन्रुन् मलरटि पणि तमियनै तविक्कविडामल्
उन्नरुळतोर् तुणै इनि उलकिल् इल्लये
एन्तन् मुन्नवने यानैमुखने मुरुकनुक्करुळं तुतिक्कैयाने
मुक्कर्परन् मकने विघ्न विनायकने
मुक्कनि मोदक प्रियने अभयमभयं विरैन्तु वन्तरुळ्।।

taruṇamidaiyā dayai puri tutikkaiyā uriya
śaraṇam enrun malaraṭi paṇi tamiyanai tavikka viḍāmal
unnaruḷator tuṇai ini ulakil illaye
entan munnavane yānaimukhane muruganu kkaruḷam tutikkaiyāne
mukkarparanmakane vighnavināyakane
mukkanimodakapriyane abhayamabhayam viraintu vantaruḷ.

3. Tarunamidayyã dayai puri

O Lord! This is the right moment for showing compassion,
O Lord whose hand is the trunk!
Without refusing this servant who has sought refuge at your flower-like feet,
This is the right moment to show compassion!
Other than your blessing, I have no other help in this world,
O my Master! O elephant-faced One who helped Subrahmania,
O Lord whose hand is the trunk!
O son of the three-eyed Lord, Siva!
O Lord of obstacles, who have no leader above you!
O Lord who are fond of the three fruits (mango, jackfruit, banana) and the rice cake,
Come soon and give me fear-free refuge!

राग: रीतिगौळ Raga: Rītigowḷa

4. तत्त्वमऱिय तरमा - मूलाधार गणपते - सुरपते - उनतु
सत्त्वगुणमुं जीवद्यैयुं - ज्ञानमुं
चट्ट्रुमिल्लात किरातनुक्कुनतु
मधुरपरिपूर्ण मोदक करने
महा विघ्नवन कुटार वरने
निधि योन्पतुं अन्पर्क्करुळ् परने
निखिल चराचर बीजाङ्कुरने
मतिशेखरन् मकने सुमुखने
मद वारण मुखने
श्रुति मुटिवुणर्वरु चित्परने - गुहसोदरने
रामदासनुक्कुनतु—तत्त्वमरिय तरमा।।

tattvamariya taramā mūlādhāragaṇapate surapate unatu
sattvaguṇamum jīvadyaiyum jnānamum
caṭṭrumillāta kirātanukkunatu
madhuraparipūrṇamodakakarane
mahā vighnavanakuṭāravarane
nidhiyonpatum anparkkaruḷparane
nikhila carācara bījāṇkurane
matiśekharanmakane sumukhane
madavāraṇamukhane
śrutimuṭivuṇarvarucitparane guhasodarane
rāmadāsanukkunatu—tattvamariya taramā.

4. Tatvamariya taramã

Am I fit to understand your Truth? O Lord of spiritual attendants located in the Muladhara, O Lord of angels! How can this wild being (which I am), who has no good quality like Sattva, no compassion for living beings, and no knowledge at all, understand your truth?

O Lord full of total sweetness, who hold the rice cake in your hand,

O great supreme Lord who is the axe for the forest of obstacles,

O supreme one, who grant the nine treasures to devotees!

Who are the seed for all beings movable and immobile, O son of the crescent crested Lord, Siva, O pleasant faced Lord! O elephant-faced One!

O lord who understand the essence of Vedanta, O brother of Subrahmania,

Is this Ramadasa fit to understand your Truth?

राग: श्री रंजनी

Raga: Shrī Ranjanī

5. गजवदन करुणासदन
शंकर बाला लम्बोदर सुंदर
अजन मरेन्द्रनुं मुनिवरुं पणि पङ्-
कज चरणं शरणं शरणं श्री
नीये मूवुलकिर्काधारं
नीये शिवागम मन्त्रसारं
नीये वाऴ्विलेन् जीवाधारं
नीयरुळ्वाय् सुमुख ओंकार—गजवदन।।

gajavadana karuṇāsadana
śamkarabālā lambodarasundara
ajanamarendranum munivarum paṇi pan–
kajacaraṇam śaraṇam śaraṇam śrī
nīye mūvulakirkādhāram
nīye śivāgamamantrasāram
nīye vāzhvilen jīvādhāram
nīyaruḷvāy sumukha omkāra—gajavadana.

5. Gajavadana Karunasadana

O elephant-faced Lord! O abode of compassion!
O son of Sankara, the Creator of bliss!
O handsome Lord with the big belly!
Your lotus feet at which bow Brahma, Indra and superior sages, are my refuge, my refuge!
You alone are the support of the three worlds!
You are the essence of all the auspicious scriptures and mantras pertaining to Siva,
You alone are the life support in my life!
Bless me, O pleasant faced Lord who are the Pranava sound, AUM!

राग: देवमनोहरि Raga: Devamanohari

6. श्री गणपतिये तिरुवरुळ् तन्तरुळ् इत्ततिये
आगम मऱैमुतलां पल कलैकट्
कादि परं पोरुळ् आकुमेकने आकुवाहने
निन्नरुळिन्ऱि ययनुं चेयुं विनैयुं
निऱैवुरुमो इटैयूट्टुमो यान्
एन् निनैवोडु मोऴितन्निलुं तोऴिलिलुं
इन्नल् विरवि इरुळ् तुन्ऱु नेरि चेन्ऱु
पोन्ऱातु मुन्निन्ऱु—श्री गणपतिये।।

śrī gaṇapatiye tiruvaruḷ tantaruḷ ittatiye
āgamamaraimutalām palakalaikaṭ
kādiparamporuḷ ākumekane ākuvāhane
ninnaruḷinriyayanum ceyum vinaiyum
niraivurumo iṭaiyūṭṭrumo yān
en ninaivoḍu mozhitannilum tozhililum
innal viravi iruḷ tunru neri cenru
ponrātu munninru—śrī gaṇapatiye.

6. Sri Ganapatiye

O auspicious Lord of spiritual attendants!
Grant your grace now itself!
You are mentioned in the Vedas and other scriptures as the primal One!
You are the supreme One, lording over many arts!
You are unique! O Lord who ride the mouse!
Without your grace, can any action I do reach completion?
Remember me and in all that I speak and do,
Remove ignorance and enforce righteousness and bless me, appearing before me!
O auspicious Lord of spiritual attendants!

राग: खरहरप्रिय　　　Raga: Kharaharapriya

7. गणपतिये करुणानिधिये
कटैक्कण् पार्त्तरुळे श्री महा
तुणैयटि तोऴुं अन्पर् तुयर् तुटैक्कुं तुय्या
सुन्दर चरणारविन्द तुतिक्कैया
सकल सुरासुरर् पणिमलर्प्पदने
शंकरन् उमैयुं मनमकिऴ् सुतने
जगं मुऴुतुं निऱै यानैमुखवने
ताळ् पणिन्तेन् तञ्चं नीये भगवने—गणपतिये।।

ganapatiye karuṇānidhiye
kaṭaikkaṇ pārttaruḷe śrī mahā
tuṇaiyaṭi tozhum anpar tuyar tuṭaikkum tuyyā
sundara caraṇāravinda tutikkaiyā
sakala surāsurar paṇimalarppadane
śankaranumaiyum manamakizh sutane
jagam muzhutum niṛai yānaimukhavane
tāḷ paṇinten tancam nīye bhagavane—gaṇapatiye.

7. Ganapatiye Karuṇānidhiye

O Lord of spiritual attendants! treasurehouse of compassion!

Bless me with your glance, O great Lord of spiritual attendants!

O Lord who wipe away the distress of devotees who bow to your feet which are a source of help.

O Lord whose hand is the trunk, your lotus feet are beautiful!

All the celestials bow at your flower-like feet!

O son who gladden the hearts of Sankara and Uma!
O elephant-faced one, who pervade the entire universe!

O resplendent Lord! I fall at your feet! You are my only refuge!

राग: मध्यमावति   Raga: Madhyamāvati

8. विघ्न विनायक मूर्त्तिक्कु मंगलं
वेऴैमुखमोडु तवऴ्
अग्निवैत्त नेट्ट्रिक्कण्णनुं आदिपराशक्ति अन्नैयुं
एन् मकन् एन् मकन् एन्ऱु
मटि वैत्तु क्कोञ्चि विळयाडुं अञ्चुकरबाल
ओरु पकैयिल्लाद उत्तम दैवं
उम्पर् मुनिवर् पणि गणपतिदैवं
विरि चराचरादि मूलमाय् मिळिर्
विधि विष्णु शिवाकारमाय ओळिर्
विघ्न विनायक मूर्त्तिक्कु मंगलं।।

vighnavināyakamūrttikku mangalam
vezhaimukhamoḍu tavazh
agnivaittaneṭṭrikkaṇṇanum ādiparāśakti annaiyum
en makan en makan enru
maṭivaittukkoncivilayāḍum ancukarabāla
orupakaiyillāda uttama daivam
umpar munivar paṇi gaṇapatidaivam
viricarācarādimūlamāy miḷir
vidhiviṣṇuśivākāramāy oḷir
vighna vināyaka mūrttikku mangalam.

8. Vighna Vināyaka Mūrtikku

Auspicious prostrations to the Lord of obstacles, who has no leader above him!

Who shines with the elephant face!

Auspicious prostrations to

the five-handed son who is petted on the lap by the Lord whose eye in the forehead is fire (Siva) and the primordial power (the Divine Mother),

saying my son, my son!

the noble Lord who harbours no ill-feeling!

the Lord of spiritual attendants, who is worshipped by angels and sages,

who has the greatness of being the cause of varied life,

that which moves and does not move,

the Lord who shines in the forms of Brahma, the Creator, Visnu, the Preserver, and Siva, the Destroyer.

Auspicious valedictory prostrations!